*1*

# *LITTLE RED*
# *WRITING*
# *BOOK*

DELUXE EDITION

# THE
# LITTLE RED
# *WRITING*
# *BOOK*

## DELUXE EDITION

Two Winning Books in One
WRITING *plus* GRAMMAR

# BRANDON ROYAL

Maven Publishing

Published by:

Maven Publishing
4520 Manilla Road
Calgary, Alberta, Canada  T2G 4B7
www.mavenpublishing.com

Library and Archives Canada Cataloguing in Publication:

Royal, Brandon, author
The little red writing book deluxe edition: two winning books in one, writing plus grammar / Brandon Royal.

Includes bibliographical references and index.
Issued in print and electronic formats.

ISBN 978-1-897393-25-3 (paperback)
ISBN 978-1-897393-27-7 (ebook)

1. English language--Rhetoric. 2. English language--Style.
3. Report writing. 4. English language--Grammar.
I. Royal, Brandon. Little gold grammar book. II. Title.

PE1408.R6795 2012      808'.042      C2012-900737-4

Cover Design: George Foster, Fairfield, Iowa, USA

This book's cover text was set in Minion.
The interior text was set in Scala and Scala Sans.

# Contents

## Part III: Readability

## Part IV: Grammar

# Preface

This deluxe edition contains the complete contents of *The Little Red Writing Book* and *The Little Gold Grammar Book*. Whereas writing is based on principles—in which writing is deemed better or worse, more effective or less effective—grammar is based on rules in which writing is deemed right or wrong, correct or incorrect. With coverage of the most useful writing principles and the most commonly encountered rules of grammar, *The Little Red Writing Book Deluxe Edition* is an invaluable guide for anyone who wants to master those skills that will make a good writer even better.

# Introduction

This book is based on a simple but powerful observation: Students and young professionals who develop outstanding writing skills do so primarily by mastering a limited number of the most important writing principles and grammar rules, which they use over and over again. What are these recurring principles and rules? The answer to this question is the basis of this material.

Writing has four pillars—structure, style, readability, and grammar—and each pillar is like the single leg of a sturdy chair. Structure is about organization and deciding in which order to present your ideas. Style describes how one writes, including how to use specific examples to support what is written. Readability is about presentation and how to make a document visually pleasing and easy to read. Grammar, including diction, is about expressing language in a correct and acceptable form.

Given the pervasive nature of writing, this guidebook is suitable for a wide-ranging audience, including writing aficionados from all walks of life. High school and college students can use this material for supplementary study. Businesspersons can use this material as a refresher course. Individuals preparing for job placement tests and students preparing for college or graduate entrance exams will benefit from a time-tested review of basic writing principles and rules.

Let's get started.

# Part I

# Structure

*I'm sorry to have written such a long letter. If I had had more time, I could have written a shorter one.*

—Blaise Pascal

# Principle 1

## Write With a Top-Down Approach

☞ Principle #1:    Write your conclusion and place it first.

Writing done for everyday purposes falls into the category of expository writing, which includes newspaper articles, college essays, and business memos and letters. Expository writing explains and often summarizes a topic or issue. Strategically, the summary or conclusion should come at the beginning of an expository piece, not at the end. The reader is first told what the writing is about, then given the supporting facts or details. This way, the reader is not left guessing at the writer's main idea.

Whereas the primary purpose of expository writing is to explain, inform, or persuade, the primary purpose of fiction or creative writing is to enlighten or entertain. As far as fiction and creative writing are concerned, it is fine (even desirable) to delay the conclusion, as in the case of a surprise ending. But the hard-and-fast rule in expository writing is that we should not keep our conclusion from the reader. We should come out with it right away. When our purpose is to explain or inform, don't play, "I've got a secret."

Experienced writing instructors know that one of the easiest ways to fix students' writing is to have them place their conclusions near the top of the page, not the bottom. Instructors are fond of a trick that involves asking students to write a short piece on a random topic and, upon completion, walking up to each student without reading what he or she has written, circling the last sentence, and moving it to the very top of the page. In a majority of cases, instructors know that the last lines written contain the conclusion. This technique is known as BLOT, or "bottom line on top." It is human nature, and it seems logical, that we should conclude at the end rather than the beginning. But writing should be top-down, structured in the inverted pyramid style. The broad base of the inverted pyramid is analogous to the broad conclusion set forth at the beginning of a piece.

Favor the top-down approach to writing:

# Most Important☺

## Next Most Important

### Next Most Important

#### Least Important

Avoid the bottom-up approach to writing:

**Least Important**

**Next Most Important**

**Next Most Important**

# Most Important☹

The newspaper industry depends upon the top-down technique of writing. Reporters know that if their stories cannot fit into the allocated space, their editors will cut from the bottom up. Therefore, conclusions generally cannot appear in the last lines, which are reserved for minor details.

Errors of writing often mimic errors in conversation. When we write, we should think about giving the reader a destination first before giving him or her the directions on how to get there. If we fail to do this, we will not get our message across in the most effective way. The value of a top-down approach in real life conversation occurs in the following dialogue.

POOR VERSION

Dialogue between two coworkers:

*"Alice, can you do something for me when you're downtown? If you're taking the subway to Main Street, get off and take the first exit out of the subway and walk down to Cross Street. At the intersection of Cross Street and Vine, you'll find Sandy's Stationery Store. <u>Can you go in and pick up a pack of Pentel 0.5mm lead refills?"</u>*

BETTER VERSION

Dialogue between two coworkers:

*Alice, can you do something for me when you're downtown? <u>I need a pack of Pentel 0.5mm lead refills.</u> The best place to get them is Sandy's Stationery Store. You can take the subway to Main Street, get off and take the first exit out of the subway and walk down to Cross Street. The store is at the intersection of Cross Street and Vine.*

The conclusion is underlined in each version. Note how annoying the first version can be from the listener's perspective. If you have encountered a similar situation in everyday life, you may have felt like screaming. Once you finally find out what the speaker's point is, you might have to ask him or her to repeat everything so you can remember the details. The same holds true for writing. It is just as frustrating when you are reading a piece of writing and you do not know where the discussion is going.

Conceptually, we want to think in terms of a descending writing structure—one in which we move "downhill" from conclusion to details rather than "uphill" from details to conclusion.

Compare the following two versions of the same piece of business writing. In evaluating the two samples, we find that the second one is more top-down in its approach. The conclusion is at the top: "Asia and Africa represent the biggest future international market for basic consumer goods if population is used as a measure." Also, the second version uses statistics solely as detail.

LESS EFFECTIVE

*Three-fourths of the world's people currently live in Asia and Africa— from South Africa to the Sahara, from the Middle East to Japan, from Siberia to Indonesia. This population statistic is quite revealing. If we selectively and representatively choose four persons from the entire world, here is what the probable outcome would be. One person would be from China, one would be from India, and one more would* be from somewhere else in Asia or Africa. The fourth person would have to be chosen from all of North America, South America, Europe, and Oceania!

Basic consumer goods represent durable and nondurable daily necessities, including food and cooking utensils, clothing and textiles, toiletries, electronics, home furnishings, and mechanized and miscellaneous household products. _Hence, Asia and Africa represent the biggest future international market for basic consumer goods if population is used as a measure._

## MORE EFFECTIVE

_Asia and Africa represent the biggest future international market for basic consumer goods if population is used as a measure._ Basic consumer goods represent durable and nondurable daily necessities, including food and cooking utensils, clothing and textiles, toiletries, electronics, home furnishings, and mechanized and miscellaneous household products.

Three-fourths of the world's people currently live in Asia and Africa—from South Africa to the Sahara, from the Middle East to Japan, from Siberia to Indonesia. This population statistic is quite revealing. If we selectively and representatively choose four persons from the entire world, here is what the probable outcome would be. One person would be from China, one would be from India, and one more would be from somewhere else in Asia or Africa. The fourth person would have to be chosen from all of North America, South America, Europe, and Oceania!

Now review this piece:

Hundreds of people packed into the auditorium seats on the evening of December 29. Being one of twelve opening performers, I was granted the opportunity to dance on stage for the first time in my life. Although my part only lasted five minutes, those five minutes became a significant moment in my life. Ever since rehearsals began two months before, I had spent many hours practicing on my own, in addition to the normal rehearsal sessions. Whether on a bus, waiting in a doctor's office, or walking to work, I always had my MP3 player *on, listening to the music and trying to go through the steps in my mind over and over again. I was determined to do my best. <u>Despite my best preparation, my nervousness caused me to slip during the performance.</u> All of a sudden, my mind turned blank. I stood there, not knowing how to react to the music. Fifteen seconds seemed like 15 hours in a normal day.*

The conclusion as underlined above is either well placed or ill placed depending on the writer's purpose in writing the passage. If the purpose is to inform the reader, then it is ill placed because the conclusion should be placed nearer the top. But as this is likely a creative writing piece, meant to entertain, the conclusion can be delayed. Just remember the rule of expository writing that governs everyday writing: Your conclusion should be at or very near the beginning of your written piece.

> An airline pilot never leaves the runway without having a destination and flight pattern. When our purpose in writing is to explain or inform, we should conclude first then concentrate on supporting details. Don't play "I've got a secret."

# Principle 2

## Break Things Down

👉 Principle #2:   Break your subject into two to four major parts and use a lead sentence.

Assuming that you know what you want to write about, you must decide what basic building blocks will comprise your work. You can break your subject into two to four major parts. Three parts are typically recommended, but for the sake of simplicity, no more than four categories should be introduced. The classic "five-paragraph" approach to writing can be used to outline, in one paragraph, any writing piece. In the example on page 21, all you have to do is supply the colors!

## LEAD SENTENCES VS. TOPIC SENTENCES

Once you have broken down your topic into two to four major categories, next you will want to elaborate on these ideas. Consider using a *lead sentence*, which is similar to a *topic sentence*. Whereas a topic sentence summarizes the contents of a single paragraph within an essay or report, a lead sentence summarizes the contents of an entire essay or report. Placed at the beginning of a piece, it foreshadows what is to come, highlighting what items will be discussed and, typically, the order in which they will be discussed. Each item in the lead should be developed into at least one separate paragraph within the body of the essay or report. For example, in a personal essay, this sentence could serve as an introduction or lead:

*I would like to show who I am through a discussion of three special turning points in my personal and career development: when I went to university on a lacrosse scholarship, when I spent a year with the Peace Corps, and when I joined a commodity trading firm in London.*

In a business report, the following could serve as a lead sentence, placed at the beginning of a report:

*Based on information taken from a recent survey, this report summarizes the three biggest problems that our company faces: namely, employee turnover, store thefts, and poor customer service.*

The number three is a magic number in writing. Think of building your writing around three key ideas or concepts.

# FINDING TWO TO FOUR MAJOR IDEAS

## Introduction

Colors make the world bright and full. My favorite colors are green, blue, and yellow. Each of these colors is special to me.

_____

_____

_____.

## Body

Green is like the green grass that blankets the earth _____

_____

_____

_____.

Blue is like the sky that soars high above. _____

_____

_____

_____.

Yellow is like the sun that shines so brightly. _____

_____

_____

_____.

## Conclusion

Green is the most interesting of all these colors. Even the colors blue and yellow combine to form green. _____

_____

_____

_____.

## OUTLINES FOR BUSINESS REPORT WRITING

The following page contains sample outlines for the four classic types of business reports. Although it is useful to think of all expository writing as having an introduction, body, and conclusion, in the case of business reports, the word "findings" is typically substituted for the word "body." Note though that the "findings" section, as shown on the next page, is broken down into three to four categories. Business reports include executive summaries (usually one page) and recommendations (usually two pages). An executive summary is "a summary of the writer's findings, conclusions, and recommendations." It comes first in the report but is written last. A recommendation is "a statement of what the writer thinks should be done as a result of his or her conclusions."

Business reports can serve one of four purposes: (1) feasibility study, (2) comparative study, (3) evaluation study, and (4) cost study. One way to summarize the differences among these reports is to take a hypothetical example from the world of business. Let's choose the Wonderland Hotel chain, which is considering expanding its operations to Jakarta, Indonesia. First, a *feasibility study report* is required. Executives at the head office must ask, "Is the hotel market in Jakarta sufficiently large enough to ensure that our hotel can prosper?" Next, assuming the hotel is built and operational, executives at regional headquarters may ask: "How do operations, including revenues, expenses, and profits, compare between the Singapore Wonderland Hotel and the Jakarta Wonderland Hotel?" This question forms the basis of a *comparative study report*. Next, the manager of the Jakarta Wonderland Hotel, who wants to increase hotel service to its customers, issues a questionnaire for guests to fill out. The questionnaire, titled "Are You Satisfied?," forms the basis of an *evaluation study report*. Finally, the manager of the Jakarta Wonderland Hotel, based on results from its survey, seeks authorization to build a water slide, games room, and reading room—all things that guests say they want. How much will it cost to build a water slide, games room and reading room? This question forms the basis of a *cost study report*.

# Feasibility Study Report   Comparative Study Report

Executive Summary

Contents

Introduction

Findings

   2.1 Size of the market
   2.2 Competitors
   2.3 Market entry strategy
   2.4 Financing of operations

Conclusions

Recommendations

Appendixes

Executive Summary

Contents

Introduction

Findings

   2.1 Revenue analysis
   2.2 Expense analysis
   2.3 Profit analysis

Conclusions

Recommendations

Appendixes

# Evaluation Study Report   Cost Study Report

Executive Summary

Contents

Introduction

Findings

   2.1 Questionnaire
   2.2 Evaluation of customer
      ratings from 1 to 5
   2.3 Evaluation of written
      responses

Conclusions

Recommendations

Appendixes

Executive Summary

Contents

Introduction

Findings

   2.1 Water slide
   2.2 Games room
   2.3 Reading room

Conclusions

Recommendations

Appendixes

# Principle 3

## Use Transition Words

👉 Principle #3: Use transition words to signal the flow of your writing.

"Transition" words, such as *but* and *however*, have been called the traffic lights of language. They serve one of four primary purposes: to show contrast, illustration, continuation, or conclusion. On the next page, you will see transition words highlighted in two sample paragraphs. Words of illustration include *first, second, for instance*, and *for example*. *So* signals conclusion. *However* signals contrast. *Moreover* signals continuation.

Transition words appear underlined in the following examples.

## EXAMPLE 1

*Time management involves thinking in terms of effectiveness <u>first</u> and efficiency <u>second</u>. <u>Whereas</u> efficiency is concerned with doing a task in the fastest possible manner, effectiveness is concerned with spending time doing the "right" things. Effectiveness is <u>therefore</u> a broader, more useful concept, which questions whether we should even do a particular task.*

## EXAMPLE 2

*The process of evolution takes two distinct forms: organic and exosomatic. In the <u>first</u>, which is commonly called Darwinian evolution, a plant or animal develops a genetic mutation that may be either helpful or harmful. If the change is helpful, the organism is favored by the process of natural selection and flourishes; if it is harmful, the organism suffers and eventually dies out.*

*The whole of what we call human culture, <u>on the other hand</u>, is a result of exosomatic evolution. Such a change may be gradual, <u>but</u> it represents conscious choices that enable human beings to adapt to environments that would otherwise be inimical to their survival.*

## EXAMPLE 3

*How does the world's deadliest snake differ from the world's most dangerous snake? The world's deadliest snake is the one that is the most venomous <u>while</u> the world's most dangerous snake is the one that kills the most people. <u>Undoubtably</u>, the Belcher Sea Snake is the world's deadliest; a few milligrams of its venom can kill 1,000 people. This docile snake, <u>however</u>, rarely comes into contact with humans.*

*The Carpet Viper kills the most people each year <u>so</u> it is considered the world's most dangerous snake. Some 20,000 people living throughout Africa and Asia lose their lives to this snake species each year.*

*<u>Coincidentally</u>, what is the world's most feared snake? This "title" is likely held by the Black Mamba. Africa's longest and fastest snake, this highly venomous, ill-tempered, and unpredictable snake is known to attack even when not provoked.*

## THE FOUR TYPES OF TRANSITION WORDS

**I. Continuation Words**

**GREEN LIGHT**
"Keep going in the same direction"

*Examples:*
•moreover •furthermore
•on the one hand
•undoubtedly
•coincidentally

**II. Illustration Words**

**FLASHING GREEN**
"Slow down and be watchful"

*Examples:*
•first, second, third
•for example •for instance •in fact
•case in point

**III. Contrast Words**

**FLASHING YELLOW**
"Get ready to turn"

*Examples:*
•however
•but •yet
•on the other hand
•whereas •while
•conversely

**IV. Conclusion Words**

**RED LIGHT**
"You're about to arrive"

*Examples:*
•in conclusion
•finally •clearly
•hence •so •thus
•therefore
•as a result

EXERCISE

Read the sentences below, arranging them in a manner that makes the most sense in terms of logic and flow. You'll find the suggested solutions on page 115.

TOPIC: THE WHALE

1. When people think of ants, on the other hand, they tend to think of hardworking, underfed creatures, transporting objects twice their body size to and from hidden hideaways.

2. When most people think of whales, they think of sluggish, obese animals, frolicking freely in the ocean and eating tons of food to sustain themselves.

3. In fact, when we compare the proportionate food consumption of all living creatures, we find that the whale is one of the most food-efficient creatures on earth.

4. However, if we analyze food consumption based on body size, we find that ants eat their full body weight every day, while a whale eats the equivalent of only one-thousandth of its body weight each day.

5. The whale is the largest mammal in the animal kingdom.

## THE SIMPLEST WRITING APPROACH

Here is a sure-fire way to write just about anything. It might not be the most exciting writing structure, but it is clear and it works.

Instructions

1. Take a stance.
2. Write your conclusion.
3. State "There are several reasons for this."
4. Use transition words. Voilà.

## EXAMPLE TOPIC: RENAISSANCE

The Renaissance period was the most glorious time in human history. There are several reasons for this. First, \_\_\_

_____Second, _____

_____Third, _____

_____For instance, _____

_____Moreover_____

_____Finally, _____

_____.

# Principle 4

## Review the Six Basic Writing Structures

👉 **Principle #4:** Use the six basic writing structures to put ideas in their proper order.

Writing is very much about the order of ideas presented and the emphasis given to them. In terms of order, we expect ideas to unfold logically, which typically means seeing the most important ideas first. In terms of emphasis, we expect the most important ideas to get the most coverage. The six commonly used structures in writing include: (1) categorical, (2) evaluative, (3) chronological, (4) comparative, (5) sequential, and (6) causal.

The emphasis or weight given to ideas is important in all structures. The more you write about something, the more important that idea or topic is deemed to be. Order is also important, but not of paramount importance in all cases. Structures in which order is important include chronological, comparative, sequential, and causal structures. In chronological structures, you discuss the earliest events first and move forward in time. In comparative structures, the most important ideas come before any others. In sequential structures, you begin with the first item in a sequence and end with the last item in the sequence. In cause-and-effect structures, causes are usually identified and discussed before their effects.

In other structures, order is less important. These include categorical and evaluative structures. If we choose to structure our writing by category, it will not make much difference whether we talk about America, China, and then Britain, or start with Britain, go on to China, and finish with America. The same is true with structures based on evaluation; it generally makes little difference whether we discuss pros first and cons second or cons first and pros last. Moreover, if the writer wants to emphasize one side more than the other (or one idea more than another), he or she should make sure the conclusion does this.

Although not considered classic writing structures, two other common writing formats include "Question and Answer" and "Problem and Solution." These structures tend to be less formal, and are often used with memos, handouts, and flyers.

NOTE ❧ Writing structures relate to the body of a writing piece, not to the introduction or conclusion.

> Zoology 101: You can tell what kind of animal it is by looking at the skeleton. Structure informs content. Important ideas in writing demand the most attention and get discussed first.

## SUMMARY OF THE SIX WRITING STRUCTURES

| | Structure | Proper Order | Examples |
|---|---|---|---|
| 1 | **Categorical**<br><br>• Item 1, item 2, item 3<br>• A, B or B, A<br>• A, B, C or C, B, A | • Discuss items in any order. | **2 items**<br>• Let's talk about apples and oranges.<br><br>**3 items**<br>• Let's talk about America, China, and Britain. |
| 2 | **Evaluative**<br><br>• Pros and cons<br>• Positives and negatives<br>• Pluses and minuses | • Discuss the pro-side first, then the con-side (or vice versa). | **2 items**<br>• Let's talk about the weather: sunny but humid.<br><br>**3 items**<br>• Let's talk about what voters think: those for, those against, and those undecided. |
| 3 | **Chronological**<br><br>• Past, present, future<br>• Before, during, after | • Discuss early events first, followed by later events. | **2 items**<br>• Let's talk about sales from January to June.<br><br>**3 items**<br>• Let's talk about Europe's economy: 1800s, 1900s, and the year 2000 and beyond. |

| | Structure | Proper Order | Examples |
|---|---|---|---|
| 4 | **Comparative**<br><br>• A > B; B > A<br>• C > B > A<br>• C > A or B | • Discuss most relevant contrasting features first; discuss less important features next. | **2 items**<br>• Let's discuss our most important goals and our minor goals.<br><br>**3 items**<br>• Let's compare our company to our competitors' size, products, and people/resources. |
| 5 | **Sequential**<br><br>• 1st, 2nd, 3rd<br>• X to Y to Z (or reverse) | • Discuss items in order of sequence, from first to last (or in reverse). | **2 items**<br>• Let's discuss drug addiction that progresses from soft drugs to hard drugs.<br><br>**3 items**<br>• Let's talk about lawmaking at the municipal, state, and national levels. |
| 6 | **Causal**<br><br>• A leads to B<br>• A and B lead to C<br>• A → B<br>• A + B → C | • Discuss early events first, followed by later events (or vice versa). | **2 items**<br>• Let's talk about whether the increase in unemployment is the cause of the increase in crime.<br><br>**3 items**<br>• Let's talk about the primary causes of global warming, the likely effects of global warming, and the controversy surrounding the issue. |

## OUTLINES FOR THE SIX WRITING STRUCTURES

The following are sample outlines highlighting the six types of writing structures.

**CATEGORICAL**

Introduction

Let's discuss three countries.

America ...

China ...

Britain ...

Conclusion

**COMPARATIVE**

Introduction

Let's compare our company to our competitors.

In terms of size ...

In terms of products and services ...

In terms of people and resources ...

Conclusion

**EVALUATIVE**

Introduction

Let's evaluate what voters think.

Those for our party ...

Those against our party ...

Those still undecided ...

Conclusion

**SEQUENTIAL**

Introduction

Let's discuss lawmaking hierarchy at three levels.

At the municipal level ...

At the state level ...

At the national level ...

Conclusion

**CHRONOLOGICAL**

Introduction

Let's discuss the economy of Europe.

In the 1800s ...

In the 1900s ...

In the year 2000 and beyond ...

Conclusion

**CAUSAL**

Introduction

Let's discuss the primary causes and likely effects of global warming.

The primary causes are ...

The likely effects are ...

The controversy is ...

Conclusion

Below are two representative samples of "Question and Answer" and "Problem and Solution" formats. One you might find as part of a travel brochure; the other you might find as part of a business memo.

## QUESTION AND ANSWER EXAMPLE

Question:    *What is the best way to visit another country?*

Answer:    *Take only pictures and leave only footprints.*

Question:    *How can we help protect endangered animals?*

Answer:    *Fight against loss of animal habitat, prosecute poachers, and prohibit the sale or purchase of endangered animals and their by-products.*

## PROBLEM AND SOLUTION EXAMPLE

During our annual conference, many corporate issues were raised. Here is a list of problems cited and our proposed solutions.

Problem:    *High employee turnover.*

Solution:    *Put more effort into recruiting; establish an in-house training program; institute weekly happy hours each Friday, paid for by the company.*

Problem:    *Increased marketplace competition.*

Solution:    *Redefine our company focus; discontinue products and product lines that fail the 80-20 rule; hold employee brainstorming sessions in hopes of finding new ideas and creative solutions.*

# Principle 5

## Keep Like Things Together

👉 **Principle #5:** Finish discussing one topic before going on to discuss other topics.

Imagine visiting the zoo to find that all the animals were in one big cage. It would not only be dangerous for the animals but also nearly impossible for visitors to view the animals in a coherent manner. Unfortunately, sometimes a piece of writing can be like a zoo, in which all of the different animals (ideas) are in one big cage, running wild. When we write (as when we speak), the ideas we describe should be grouped together. It is best to finish discussing one idea before going on to discuss another.

Here's an example of an essay with jumbled ideas.

## ORIGINAL VERSION

*In 1981, Roger Sperry received the Nobel Prize for his proof of the split-brain theory. According to Dr. Sperry, the brain has two hemispheres with different, but overlapping functions.*

*The left side of the brain is responsible for analytical, linear, verbal, and rational thought. Left-brain thinking is "spotlight" thinking. The right hemisphere is holistic, imaginative, nonverbal, and artistic. It is the left brain that a person relies on when balancing a checkbook, remembering names and dates, or setting goals and objectives. Whenever a person recalls another person's face, becomes engrossed in a symphony, or simply daydreams, that person is engaging in right-brain functions. Right-brain thinking is "floodlight" thinking and right-brain processes are, to the chagrin of many, less often rewarded in school. Since most of the Western concepts of thinking come from Greek logic, which is a linear logic system, left-brained processes are most rewarded in the western educational system.*

*In summary, the right and left hemispheres of the brain each specialize in distinct types of thinking processes. In the most basic sense, the left brain is the analytical side while the right brain is the creative side.*

Note that although the above writing piece employs a classic structure—containing an introduction, body, and conclusion—the content is difficult to read and absorb because ideas are tangled. If this discussion were to continue for a couple of pages, the reader might feel that his or her mind had turned to spaghetti. We know that there are two things under discussion—left-brain versus right-brain thinking—but the technique with which ideas are described and supported is deficient.

## CORRECTED VERSION 1

*In 1981, Roger Sperry received the Nobel Prize for his proof of the split-brain theory. According to Dr. Perry, the brain has two hemispheres with different but overlapping functions. Each hemisphere of the brain specializes in distinct types of thinking processes. In the most basic sense, the left brain is the analytical side while the right brain is the creative side.*

*The left side of the brain is responsible for analytical, linear, verbal, and rational thought. Left-brain thinking is characterized as "spotlight" thinking. It is the left brain that a person relies on when balancing a checkbook, remembering names and dates, or setting goals and objectives. The right hemisphere is holistic, imaginative, nonverbal, and artistic. Right-brain thinking is characterized as "floodlight" thinking. Whenever a person recalls another person's face, becomes engrossed in a symphony, or simply daydreams, that person is engaged in right-brain functions.*

*Since most Western concepts of thinking are derived from Greek logic, which is a linear logic system, left-brained processes are most rewarded in the Western education system. Right-brain processes are, to the chagrin of many, less often rewarded in school.*

In the corrected example above, we also have classic usage of introduction, body, and conclusion. The structure in the second paragraph proceeds as follows: left-brain thinking is described within the first two sentences, followed by a third supporting sentence which includes examples of left-brain thinking. Right-brain thinking is then described in two sentences, followed by a supporting sentence which includes examples of right-brain thinking. The third paragraph concludes with an implication of left- and right-brain thinking.

CORRECTED VERSION 2

*In 1981, Roger Sperry received the Nobel Prize for his proof of the split-brain theory. According to Dr. Perry, the brain has two hemispheres with different but overlapping functions. Each hemisphere of the brain specializes in distinct types of thinking processes. In the most basic sense, the left brain is the analytical side while the right brain is the creative side.*

*The left side of the brain is responsible for analytical, linear, verbal, and rational thought. Left-brain thinking is characterized as "spotlight" thinking. It is the left brain that a person relies on when balancing a checkbook, remembering names and dates, or setting goals and objectives. Since most Western concepts of thinking are derived from Greek logic, which is a linear logic system, left-brained processes are most rewarded in the Western education system.*

*The right hemisphere is holistic, imaginative, nonverbal, and artistic. Right-brain thinking is characterized as "floodlight" thinking. Whenever a person recalls another person's face, becomes engrossed in a symphony, or simply daydreams, that person is engaged in right-brain functions. Right-brain processes are, to the chagrin of many, less often rewarded in school.*

The three-paragraph structure above is also a classic one: an introduction is followed by two paragraphs, each dedicated entirely to either left- or right-brain thinking. In the second paragraph, left-brain thinking is described within the first two sentences, followed by a third supporting sentence containing examples of this type of thinking, and a concluding sentence highlighting an implication of left-brain thinking. In the third paragraph, right-brain thinking is described in two sentences, followed by a supporting sentence with examples of this type of thinking, and finally a one sentence implication of right-brain thinking.

# Part II

# Style

When Calvin Coolidge
was asked by his wife what the
preacher had preached on, he
replied "Sin," and, when asked
what the preacher had said,
replied "He was against it." Mr.
Coolidge was brief but one hardly
envies Mrs. Coolidge.

—F.L. Lucas

# Principle 6

## Support What You Say

🖝 **Principle #6:** **Use specific and concrete words to support what you say.**

One major difference between good writing and mediocre writing lies with the specific and concrete examples that you use or fail to use. Say, for example, you are writing about an apple. Not all apples are identical. What kind of apple is it? Golden Delicious, Gala, Fuji, McIntosh, Granny Smith? What color is it? What shape is it? How does it taste? What is its texture? Where is it grown? Let's look at an example in a business context. Suppose you hear that your company's profits are down. What are the specifics? Did the sales volume decline? Was the sales price reduced? Did costs go up? And, if any of the above, then by how much?

Note the difference in each of the following statements:

GENERAL

*Corporate profits decreased.*

BETTER BUT STILL NOT SPECIFIC

*Corporate profits decreased because costs increased.*

SPECIFIC

*Corporate profits decreased by 10 percent as overall costs increased by 20 percent.*

EVEN BETTER

*Corporate profits decreased by 10 percent as overall costs increased by 20 percent. In particular, higher salary expenses were the major reason for the increase in costs. Higher salary costs were primarily the result of increases in executive compensation; the aggregate wages paid to factory workers actually decreased by 5 percent due to a decrease in the number of overtime hours clocked.*

Examples and details are the very things people remember long after reading a piece. Compare the two examples below describing the popular attitude toward science.

VERSION 1

*The popular attitude toward science in the United States is a mix of superstition and awe. Quaint folklore portrays scientific genius as solitary and requiring no nurture. Within the public imagination, such pleasant thoughts go undisturbed by the reality of today's large research labs.*

VERSION 2

*The popular attitude toward science in the United States is a mix of superstition and awe. Quaint folklore portrays scientific genius as solitary and requiring no nurture. Within the public imagination are visions of the Wright Brothers at work in their bicycle shop, contriving the first flying machine, and of Thomas Edison plumbing the mysteries of electricity with a few magnets and some pieces of wire. Such pleasant thoughts go undisturbed by today's large research labs, whose members undergo highly specialized training in order to work on narrowly defined research problems.*

The second version uses examples drawn from the Wright Brothers and Thomas Edison. This helps us visualize what the author is saying.

Consider the two memos below. Which one would convince you to attend the Calgary Stampede and Exhibition?

MEMO 1

*The Calgary Stampede will be held during the first week of July. There will be loads of activities, fun, and food for all. Bring your cowboy hat and boots. See you there!*

MEMO 2

*The Calgary Stampede will be held during the first week of July. The exhibition grounds are home to two dozen midway rides, a myriad of food stalls (try those miniature doughnuts!), the sounds of live country music, First Nations exhibits, bustling saloons, and a large casino. For the youngsters, there is a petting zoo, magic tricks, and loads of games, with the chance to win giant stuffed animals. The opening day parade has a flotilla of floats, and daily rodeo events including calf roping, bull riding, and chuck wagon races. Fantastic fireworks each evening. See you there!*

Note that the second and better example is longer than the original. Given that writing should be concise, why is the shorter example not better? A trade-off exists between brevity and detail. Sufficient detail will make a piece of writing longer, but this does not necessarily indicate wordiness. Conciseness requires a minimum number of words at the sentence level, whereas sufficient support may require more sentences.

Here is a more humorous example. Consider which of the following better demonstrates to you that a physical book is a wonderful tool.

BLURB 1

*Books are marvelous tools. They're informative and entertaining, and they are here to stay.*

BLURB 2

*The book is a revolutionary breakthrough in modern technology. No wires, no circuits, no batteries. Nothing to be connected or switched on. It's so easy, even a child can operate it. Just lift its cover! Compact and portable, it can be used anywhere—even sitting in an armchair by the fire. Yet it is powerful enough to hold as much information as a CD.*

*This is how it works: The book may be picked up at any time and used by merely opening it. The book never crashes and never needs rebooting. The browse feature allows you to move instantly to any sheet, and move forward or backward as you wish. Many come with an index feature, which pinpoints the exact location of selected information for instant retrieval. You can also make personal notes next to book entries with an optional programming tool, the Portable Erasable Nib Cryptic Intercommunication Language Stylus (PENCILS).*

*Is this the end of the computer? The BOOK (Built in Orderly Organized Knowledge) looks as though it will become the entertainment wave of the future.*

Vague language weakens your writing because it forces the reader to guess at what you mean instead of allowing him or her to concentrate fully on your ideas and style. Choose specific, descriptive words for more forceful writing. Sometimes, to be specific and concrete, you will have to use more words than usual. That's okay. While it is important to cut unnecessary words, it is even more important to properly support what you say.

### Exercise

Rewrite the following sentences to replace vague language with specific, concrete language. Suggested answers are found on pages 115–116.

1. Joannie has a dog and a cat.

2. The vacation was expensive.

3. Rainbows are colorful.

4. Sheila is tall and good-looking.

5. Many economists think that the Federal Reserve Bank is to blame for the current economic downturn.

6. Firms should advertise because advertising will surely increase sales.

7. Tim is a careless person.

8. The contestant was eliminated in the first round because she missed an easy geography question.

9. The store is packed with goods.

10. Mr. and Mrs. Jones make a cute couple.

## TRAIN YOURSELF TO CITE SPECIFIC EXAMPLES

Most writing suffers from superficiality—it is too general. Examples abound in both the academic and professional realm. For example, when writing job search letters or college application essays, candidates often write sentences such as: "I have good people skills," "I have strong communication skills," or "I have good analytical skills."

There is a debater's adage: "A statement without support merits a denial without reason." If one person says, "Purple polka-dot bikinis are awful" but gives no evidence to support the statement, another person is entitled to say, "You're wrong," and not give a reason. A valued technique, which can be used when writing rough drafts, is to stress the points you wish to make by placing "for example" immediately after what you write. This will ensure that you lend support to your statements.

NOTE ✑ As a practical matter, each writer should decide whether to leave "for example" in an essay or to edit it out, particularly if looking for a more seamless connection between ideas and support points.

The following sample sentences were taken directly from the essays of applicants applying to college or graduate school.

EXAMPLE 1

Candidate's statement:

*I am an energetic, loyal, creative, diligent, honest, strict, humorous, responsible, flexible, and ambitious person.*

Reviewer's likely comment:

*Would you care to develop your discussion and support a few of these traits with concrete examples?*

A real amateur's mistake is to use a "shopping list of traits." This could occur when you are writing to describe yourself (as is the case if writing a personal essay) or when you are writing to describe someone else (as might be the case when writing academic or professional letters of recommendation or job reference letters). Giving adequate support for a dozen traits is practically impossible. The better approach is to choose two or three traits and develop each in more detail.

EXAMPLE 2

Candidate's statement:

*Growing up in both the East and West, I have experienced both Asian and Western points of view.*

Reviewer's likely comment:

*What are these Asian and Western points of view?*

EXAMPLE 3

Candidate's statement:

*Although ABC Company did not flourish, I still consider my effort a success because I was able to identify strengths and weaknesses in my overall business skills.*

Reviewer's likely comment:

*What strengths and weaknesses did you identify?*

EXAMPLE 4

Candidate's statement:

*Not only did I develop important operational skills in running a business but I experienced and witnessed the challenges that entrepreneurs face on a daily basis.*

Reviewer's likely comment:

*What were these challenges?*

The following examples show how unsupported statements can be improved with the addition of concrete details.

ORIGINAL

*I was brought up out of context—an English girl in a British colony. I went through 13 years of international school and my primary school had twenty-eight nationalities.*

BETTER

*I was brought up out of context—an English girl in a British colony. I went through 13 years of international school and my primary school had twenty-eight nationalities. I remember when my fourth-year teacher decided to hold an International Day. Everyone wore a traditional or national costume and brought a dish of traditional cuisine. There is no real national costume for England, so I dressed as an English Rose, and brought Yorkshire Parkin, a sweet ginger cake, as my dish.*

ORIGINAL

*I grew up in a Maine farm family that was ethnically Scottish, but really your everyday New England household. I am thankful now for a stable, happy childhood. My parents gave me the best education and upbringing they could. They taught me to be caring and respectful of*

*people and the environment. They taught me honesty, humility, and
the silliness of pretense.*

BETTER

*I grew up in a Maine farm family that was ethnically Scottish, but
really your everyday New England household. I am thankful now for
a stable, happy childhood. My parents gave me the best education
and upbringing they could. They took me to museums, libraries, and
ballet lessons. They taught me to be caring and respectful of people
and the environment. Often they taught by example: When I was
four or five, my elder brothers and I accidentally lit a field on fire.
Wind caught the flames, and the fire quickly engulfed the field and
came dangerously close to our house and barn. After the fire was put
out, my parents felt our guilt and remorse and never mentioned it. We
learned the mercy of compassion and forgiveness in addition to the
foolishness of playing with matches in dry fields on windy days. My
mother taught me honesty in a different way: When we stole balloons,
she made us return them and individually admit our guilt, apologize,
and offer to pay from our birthday money (we didn't get allowances).
The humiliation of facing that storekeeper, whose sweet disposition
and insistence that we keep the balloons, which made my guilt worse,
has stayed with me until this day.*

WEAKNESSES IN SUPPORT TECHNIQUES

The next two examples are letters of recommendation (also
known as an appraisal letter), as frequently seen in the graduate
school application process, and a job reference letter. A critique
of both letters follows. In short, like so many academic and business documents, these letters could be made effective if more
specific support was given in the form of examples, quotes, or
anecdotes. In writing parlance, don't just mention the "what's,"
mention the "so what's." Mentioning the "so what's" provides
support and indicates the reason why the writer is writing about
something.

## ACADEMIC LETTER OF RECOMMENDATION

Admissions Director:

It is my pleasure to serve as a reference for Richard Tyler in his application for admission to your graduate school. I have known Richard for fourteen years, first as an associate of his father (we worked together in a large U.S. conglomerate from 2000 to 2006). Later Richard worked for me at Xerox Corporation as an accountant and financial analyst.

Richard demonstrated a high level of intelligence, strong technical skills, and a very effective and positive way of interacting with people. He quickly gained the respect and support of his peers and seniors. He made a substantial contribution at Xerox Corporation during his period of service. I would particularly like to cite his originality and desire to innovate new systems and procedures.

Another remarkable quality worthy of mention is Richard's wide range of interests—from the specific and exacting profession of accounting and quantitative analysis to the broad interests that took him to Japan for study and international experience. This is a unique range.

Based on my 32-year career in the financial management of hi-tech companies and knowledge of many applicants and young graduates over the years, I would rank Richard in the top 10 percent of his peers now applying for admission.

Sincerely,
*Frank B. Moore Jr.*
VP Finance and Chief Financial Officer
Xerox Systems of America

# JOB REFERENCE LETTER

To Whom It May Concern:

As a sales representative at the newly opened branch of Avon Cosmetic Products in Hong Kong, Judith was initially responsible for attending to the phones and walk-in customers. This was a new center for Avon International, and women's accessories was a brand new product area for the Hong Kong and PRC customers. Judith not only exceeded her sales quotas but also became our regional expert on how to adapt, modify, and package all our local products.

Besides having a very special organizational ability, Judith also has a wonderful way with her co-workers and customers. Co-workers listen to her advice and customers continue to buy from her. We have all watched Judith develop her marketing and sales skills. If she were not planning on leaving to go overseas, we would have offered her the position of director of our Beijing Avon Office, where she would not only administrate, but also train sales staff to open the China market.

As the person who started the Avon Hong Kong office and hired Judith, I am most proud of finding her for our company. She is extremely talented, diligent, and innovative, and all without formal business training. We sorely hate to lose her. I have never met another person who has greater potential to be a truly great marketer. Thus, I unqualifiedly and enthusiastically write this job reference letter. Your company will be proud of such an employee.

Sincerely,
*Elizabeth Lee*
Director, Avon Cosmetics (Hong Kong) Ltd.

## CRITIQUE OF RECOMMENDATION LETTER

This recommendation letter follows a traditional format for a graduate school letter of recommendation. It cites at a minimum the context in which the recommender knows the candidate, and a quantifiable comparison is made of the candidate to others applying to graduate school. This letter constitutes a solid endorsement; the only criticism is that it misses a few opportunities to cite details in support of things said. For example, the reviewer is likely to respond to the recommender's statement "I would particularly like to cite his originality and desire to innovate new systems and procedures" by asking for details on these new systems and procedures. Moreover, the best professional recommendations may also make mention of a candidate's career aspirations, as well as areas of needed development. Sometimes the recommender cites anecdotes or quotes that other persons have made about the applicant as additional support.

## CRITIQUE OF JOB REFERENCE LETTER

This job reference letter is a positive one, written in a light, colloquial tone. It comes across as warm and personable. A criticism of this letter lies in the lack of concrete details to support the recommender's statements. For example, the reviewer may want to know how much Judith exceeded her sales quota—by 1 percent or 200 percent—as well as the growth in sales of the Hong Kong office and how much of it should be credited to Judith's efforts. The recommender should give one example of how Judith adapted, modified, or packaged new products for the local market because the reviewer is no doubt interested. Perhaps the recommender could quote one of Judith's customers. Finally, the letter should mention one area where Judith is weak, to balance out the recommendation.

# Principle 7

## Personalize Your Examples

☛ **Principle #7:**    **Add personal examples to make your writing more memorable.**

Principle 6—use specific and concrete words to support what you say—is arguably the most important of all writing techniques. Principles 6 and 7 work in tandem and are incredibly important tools in writing as well as in speech making. Often personal examples go hand in hand with the use of the personal pronoun "I." Do not be afraid to use this pronoun; it forces the writer to relate to the topic at hand in a way that is both personal and specific. Readers appreciate knowing how a situation relates to the writer (or speaker) in terms of his or her personal experience.

For example, the statement "Nigel is too busy to enjoy himself" is a general statement. The statement "Despite working at the local Co-op during the evenings, Nigel arrives home and diligently tackles his homework to prepare for next day's classes" is a personal statement that makes the same point.

Personalizing examples makes them more memorable. The following examples will give you some idea of how to use generic and detailed support points. Detailed support points give the reader an idea of what the writer personally came away with as a result of such and such experience.

*NOTE* ⮝ In formal writing, as is the case when writing academic essays or business reports, it is standard practice to avoid the use of the personal pronoun "I." The likely reason for this is that the focus in formal writing is on the work (document) itself and not on the writer's personal opinions.

STATEMENT

*I have analytical skills.*

GENERIC SUPPORT POINT

*Analytical skills help me work with numbers to both read and interpret financial statements. Analytical skills serve as objective measures and as the basis of good decision making.*

DETAILED SUPPORT POINT

*My time spent working at Accenture Consulting helped me develop an analytical mind set. I learned to reconcile what was said verbally with its financial reality. When a client said his or her problem was high costs, I systematically broke down total costs into their individual components. Once I knew where the numbers pointed, I looked for the stories behind these numbers. Sometimes the problem was not with high costs, as the client may have thought, but with another factor in the overall system.*

STATEMENT

*People are starving.*

GENERIC SUPPORT POINT

*People are starving—you can see it in their eyes and in the way their bones press against their skin.*

DETAILED SUPPORT POINT

*But it's the faces you can't forget; like images in a recurring nightmare, they keep coming back, haunted faces, staring blankly back from the windows of tumble-down hovels. The hollow lifeless eyes, skin stretched tight across backs, hands outstretched, dull listless eyes imploring. I move as if in a dream through the agony that is famine.*

The above is an excerpt from the movie *The Year of Living Dangerously,* depicting the experiences of a young journalist stationed in Indonesia in the mid-1960s. This detailed support point also mimics the time-honored writer's adage "show, don't tell." Also, writing on an emotional level helps ensure that the reader gets a firsthand account, not a secondhand one.

Another potential weakness in support techniques occurs when students present records of extracurricular involvement when applying to college or graduate school. Because of the keen competition for entrance to highly rated schools, a candidate should present solid support for his or her involvement. Applicants often fall short, only mentioning the names of their extracurricular activities and the hours of involvement. Notice how much more meaningful a presentation becomes when a candidate not only provides proper support for what is being said but also personalizes the writing by providing detailed support points.

## PRESENTATION OF A HIGH SCHOOL EXTRACURRICULAR ACTIVITY

**Varsity Debate Team Member**
Santa Rosa High School
Sept 2010 to May 2011

**Time**
Seven to ten hours per week excluding library research and occasional weekend travel

**Description**
Competed in high school NDT debate and participated in individual speaking events; won two regional debate tournaments, Pomona Invitational and West Coast Challenge.

**Summary**
Debate taught me four things:
• to organize and defend coherent arguments
• to speak under pressure
• to develop excellent research skills
• to formulate strategies for beating tournament competitors

My time spent in debate taught me to develop affirmative and negative briefs to support and defend the resolution at hand. I learned to be ever mindful of the importance of anticipating both sides of an argument. For every argument there is an equal and opposite argument. It is here that I gained my first real insights into an old tenet of philosophy: "Only through contrast do we have awareness."

Literary techniques also can be used to strengthen your personal or even business writing. Think of these writing techniques as optional tools to support the things you say in addition to examples and statistics.

## ANECDOTES

Anecdotes are little stories used to embellish your point. For example, suppose you are writing about why we should follow our own path and not be unduly persuaded by the advice of others. You write:

*This situation reminds me of the story of a young violinist who is burdened with thoughts of whether she possesses the talent to continue playing the violin and reach her lofty goal of becoming a virtuoso. Upon a fortuitous meeting with a master violinist, the young girl asks, "Will you listen to me play and tell me if you think I have the talent to be a virtuoso?" The master then responds, "If I listen to you play, and I feel you do not have the talent, what will you do?" The girl replies, "Since I value highly your opinion, I will stop playing." The master remarks, "If you would quit because of what I would say, then you obviously do not have what it takes to be a virtuoso."*

## QUOTATIONS

Including quotations, particularly those attributed to famous or well-known people, can be a persuasive tool. Quotations, when well chosen, make you look intelligent and/or add flair to your writing piece. Unfortunately, it is not always easy to recall an applicable quote from memory, and a little research will likely be needed. In addition to books that serve as quotation collections, there are many online quotation archives.

## ANALOGIES

Analogies draw similarities between two otherwise dissimilar things and help the reader see a given relationship more clearly. For example, suppose you are writing an essay and want to stress the importance of making sales, particularly the relationship between the production department and the sales and marketing department. You might use the following "guns and bullets" analogy: "Production makes the bullets, marketing points the gun, and sales pulls the trigger." This makes clearer the idea that the production department is responsible for making products, while the marketing department is responsible for determining where sales are to be found, and the sales department is responsible for actually going out and making sales.

Say, for example, you wish to use an analogy to describe the difference between a person's personality and his or her mood swings. A climate-versus-weather analogy might be appropriate, such as: "Climate is like our fundamental personality traits, while weather is like our emotions and moods."

## SIMILES AND METAPHORS

Similes compare two unlike things and are usually introduced by "like" or "as." An example of a simile is "A sharp mind is like a knife that cuts problems open." Similes are relatively easy to use and can be powerful tools in presenting your ideas.

Metaphors literally denote that one thing is another (instead of one thing being *like* another), and the words "as" or "like" are not used. An example of a metaphor is "He has nerves of steel."

Similes and metaphors are figurative comparisons, not actual comparisons. An example of an actual comparison is "Cindy is taller than Susan." Even though the focus of this book is on expository writing—and the use of analogies, similes, and metaphors present techniques which touch on creative writing—there are still uses for such literary techniques in everyday writing. Sales letters provide an everyday business example where the use of creativity is used to grab the reader's attention.

Ponder these opening lines:

A motivational or human resource company begins a sales letter with a simile:

*Without a goal, a person is like a ship without a rudder.*

A wine distributor advertises (by analogy):

*Good wine and a good physician have one thing in common. They both can help extend your life!*

A bungee jump operator employs a metaphor:

*Do you have the heart of a lion?*

EXERCISE

Try answering the following question:

*How is a good idea like an iceberg?*

Reflect on the statement above and write several one-sentence responses. Rest assured that by coming up with a half-dozen answers to this difficult example above, you will find crafting others for everyday writing purposes just that much easier. Possible answers are listed on page 116.

> Writing should be culled, but that's not the most important task: It's the second most important aspect of writing. The most important writing principle is that ideas should be sufficiently supported. It is detail that helps to make writing believable and memorable.

# Principle 8

## Keep It Simple

☞ **Principle #8:** **Use simple words to express your ideas.**

The most fundamental way to simplify writing is to use simpler words. Simpler words—verbs, nouns, and adjectives—have broader meanings in English, while more complicated words have more specific meanings. Thus, you have a higher "margin of safety" when using simpler words.

Some writers adhere to the idea that "big words" are bad. The belief is that anyone who uses big words is just trying to impress the reader. The point embodied by Principle 8 is that the everyday writer should err on the side of using simpler words. That is not to say that there is no occasion for "bigger" or more specific vocabulary in writing, but rather that the writer should always consider how appropriate the vocabulary is for a given audience.

## USING SIMPLER WORDS

The following chart shows how we may substitute a less familiar word with one that is more familiar and, therefore, easier to understand.

| | | | |
|---|---|---|---|
| Acceded | ◌৪ Agreed | Enumerate | ◌৪ List |
| Accumulate | ◌৪ Gather | Execute | ◌৪ Carry out |
| Adaptability | ◌৪ Adapt | Facilitate | ◌৪ Make easy |
| Aggregate | ◌৪ Total | Formulate | ◌৪ Devise |
| Ameliorate | ◌৪ Improve | Implementation | ◌৪ Implement |
| Apprise | ◌৪ Tell | Locality | ◌৪ Place |
| Ascertain | ◌৪ Find out | Materialize | ◌৪ Develop |
| Attributable | ◌৪ Due | Mitigate | ◌৪ Lessen |
| Augment | ◌৪ Increase | Modification | ◌৪ Change |
| Cognizant | ◌৪ Aware | Obfuscate | ◌৪ Obscure |
| Demonstrate | ◌৪ Show | Obviate | ◌৪ Avoid |
| Diminutive | ◌৪ Tiny | Proficiency | ◌৪ Skill |
| Disseminate | ◌৪ Send out | Resourcefulness | ◌৪ Resourceful |
| Effectuate | ◌৪ Carry out | Substantiate | ◌৪ Prove |
| Endeavor | ◌৪ Try | Utilize | ◌৪ Use |

*NOTE* ◌৯ Principle 6 addressed the use of specific, concrete words as opposed to general, vague ones. Principle 8 focuses on the use of simple words. The art of writing requires that the writer reconcile these two concepts. Small words are not necessarily specific words. For example, in the following two sentences—"It's a nice house" and "The overtime period was great"—the writer should consider replacing the words "nice" and "great" with more specific ones or, alternatively, opt for additional follow-up sentences. After all, the reader will likely wonder: what does "nice" or "great" really mean?

EXERCISE

Rewrite the following sentences by expressing the ideas more simply. The suggested answers are found on page 117.

1. There is considerable evidential support for the assertion that carrot juice is good for you.

2. We anticipate utilizing hundreds of reams of recycled copy paper in the foreseeable future.

3. This plan will provide for the elimination of inefficient shipping practices.

4. Educationwise, our schoolchildren should be given adequate training in the three Rs—reading, writing, and arithmetic.

5. Only meteorologists can perform a detailed analysis of changing climatic conditions.

6. With reference to the poem, I submit that the second and third stanzas connote a certain feeling of despair.

7. That dog is the epitome, the very quintessence, of canine excellence.

8. The hurricane destroyed almost all structures along the coastline. Most homes were destroyed when a confluence of water and wind joined forces to rip off roofs and collapse walls.

9. Which point of view do I adhere to? That's a good question. While I am against war, I also realize that some situations require the use of military force.

10. Like Napoleon's army that marched on Russia more than a century before, the German army was also unable to successfully invade Russia because its soldiers were inadequately prepared for winter conditions. German soldiers didn't even have proper winter clothing to withstand the subzero temperatures.

# Principle 9

## Cut Down Long Sentences

**☞ Principle #9:** **Make your writing clearer by dividing up long sentences.**

One way to make your writing clearer is to limit the use of long sentences. The easiest way to do this is to divide a long sentence into two or more shorter sentences. Caveat: The value of using short sentences does not mean that all sentences should be short. This would create a choppy style and is precisely where the art of writing needs to come into play. The writer must judge how to weave short sentences with longer ones, as well as how to use sentence variety (see Principle 14).

Here's an example of a very long sentence that needs help.

ORIGINAL

*Leadership—whether on the battlefield or in another area, such as politics or business—can take place either by example or command, and Alexander the Great, renowned in both history and legend, is a good example of a military leader who led by both command and personal example, whereas Gandhi and Mother Teresa, both famous for their devotion to great causes, provide instances of people leading primarily by the inspiring power of personal example.*

Cutting this large sentence into at least two or three smaller sentences would result in the following:

BETTER

*Leadership can take place either by example or command. Alexander the Great is an example of a military leader who did both. Gandhi and Mother Teresa, on the other hand, led primarily by the inspiring power of personal example.*

Here is another example of a "one-sentence" paragraph:

ORIGINAL

*I entered the Neurological Faculty of the hospital and endured the next three months undergoing various diagnostic tests including EEG monitoring, in which my brain's electrical rhythms were monitored by electrodes placed on my scalp held by adhesive glue to record activity over a period of time, daily blood testing and blood counts, and all the required tests which subjected my brain to further diagnostic imaging from CAT scanning (computerized tomography), to an MRI (magnetic resonance imaging), to the costly PET scanning (positron emission tomography) and even the painful spinal fluid testing.*

Obviously the previous sentence is running wild. Cut this large sentence into two or three smaller sentences as follows:

## BETTER

*I entered the Neurological Faculty of the hospital and endured three months of diagnostic tests including EEG monitoring, daily blood testing, and blood counts. EEG monitoring subjected my brain to electrical rhythms after electrodes were attached to my scalp. Other diagnostic tests further scrutinized my brain: CAT scans (computerized tomography), MRIs (magnetic resonance imaging), costly PET scans (positron emission tomography), and even painful spinal fluid testing.*

There is power in short sentences, and their use should not be underestimated. Really short sentences (three to five words) catch the reader's eye and stand out as if naked. Their occasional use can add a dynamic touch to your writing. For example:

*I like beer. Beer explains more about me than anything in the world. Who am I? I am the beer man—at least that is what many of my close friends call me.*

One idea that carries merit is the "topic sentence, one-line rule." Topic sentences should ideally not be longer than one line to ensure that the reader grasps your point quickly.

In reference to beer and bare-naked sentences, the following sentences were used as part of a major campaign for dark beer:

*Dark is different. Dark is exquisite. Dark is discerning. Dark is determined. Dark is mysterious. Dark is sensual. Dark is smooth. Dark is the other side of one's desire.*

# Principle 10

## Eliminate Needless Words

🖝 Principle #10:     Cut out redundancies, excessive qualification, and needless self-reference.

Perhaps no one has ever captured (in 63 words!) the essence
of brevity in writing as well as William Strunk, Jr.: "Vigorous
writing is concise. A sentence should contain no unnecessary
words, a paragraph no unnecessary sentences, for the same
reason that a drawing should have no unnecessary lines and a
machine no unnecessary parts. This requires not that a writer
make all his sentences short, or that he avoid all detail and treat
his subjects only in outline, but that every word tell."

## REDUNDANCIES

Redundancy occurs when a writer needlessly repeats a word or an idea. It is redundant, for instance, to speak of an "inexperienced beginner." The word "beginner" by itself implies lack of experience. Redundant words or phrases can be eliminated without changing the meaning of the sentence.

| Redundant | Better |
| --- | --- |
| advance notice | notice |
| any and all | any |
| ask the question | question |
| attractive in appearance | attractive |
| big in size | big |
| blue in color/blue colored | blue |
| charming in character | charming |
| combined together | combined |
| completely full | full |
| consensus of opinion | consensus |
| continues to remain | continues *or* remains |
| curious in nature | curious |
| descend down | descend |
| deliberately chosen | chosen |
| end result | result |
| exceptionally outstanding | exceptional |
| few in number | few |
| final outcome | outcome |
| hope and trust | hope *or* trust |

| | |
|---|---|
| if and when | if |
| lose out | lose |
| may perhaps | may *or* perhaps |
| modern world of today | modern world |
| mutual agreement | agreement |
| new initiatives | initiatives |
| new innovation | innovation |
| past experience | experience |
| past history | history |
| positive benefits | benefits |
| reiterate again | reiterate |
| reflect back | reflect |
| repeat (over) again | repeat |
| return back | return |
| sadly tragic | tragic |
| serious crisis | crisis |
| sink down | sink |
| tall in height | tall |
| true facts/hard facts | facts |
| undergraduate student | undergraduate |
| unexpected emergency | emergency |
| unique and one-of-a-kind | unique *or* one-of-a-kind |
| unsubstantiated rumors | rumors |
| until such a time | until |
| young juvenile | juvenile |

## EXCESSIVE QUALIFICATION

Occasional use of qualifiers will let the reader know that you are reasonable, but using such modifiers too often weakens your writing. Excessive qualification makes the writer sound hesitant, and adds bulk without adding substance.

Original        *This rather serious leak may possibly shake the very foundations of the intelligence world.*

Better          *This serious leak may shake the foundations of the intelligence world.*

And there is no need to quantify words that are already absolute.

| ORIGINAL | BETTER |
|---|---|
| *fairly excellent* | *excellent* |
| *truly unique* | *unique* |
| *the very worst* | *the worst* |
| *most favorite* | *favorite* |
| *quite outstanding* | *outstanding* |

Look also for opportunities to clean out qualifiers such as *a bit, a little, highly, just, kind of, most, mostly, pretty, quite, rather, really, slightly, so, still, somewhat, sort of.* Like *very, truly,* and *fairly,* they are all weakeners and are almost always unnecessary.

## NEEDLESS SELF-REFERENCE

Avoid such unnecessary phrases as "I believe," "I feel," and "in my opinion." There is usually no need to remind your reader that what you are writing is your opinion.

Exercise 1

Rewrite the following sentences, cutting out redundancies. Suggested answers are found on page 118.

1. Attendees should be ready, willing, and able to adhere to the event's dress code and not wear casual clothes when formal attire is required.

2. A construction project that large in size needs an effective manager who can get things done.

3. The Acropolis Museum continues to remain a significant tourist attraction.

4. The ultimate conclusion is that physical and psychological symptoms are intertwined and difficult to separate.

5. The field superintendent's charisma and charming personality do not mask his scanty product or technical knowledge.

6. The recently observed trend of government borrowing may eventually create nations that are poorer and more impoverished than ever before.

7. These events—water shortages, chronic overcrowding, and rampant disease—have combined together to create a serious crisis.

8. Those who can find novel solutions to problems are few in number.

9. She has deliberately chosen to work for UNESCO.

10. Negotiation opens up many doors to peaceful settlement.

Exercise 2

Rewrite the following sentences, cutting out excessive qualification. Suggested answers appear on pages 118–119.

1. Peter is an exceptionally outstanding student.

2. You yourself are the very best person to decide what you should do with your life.

3. The propane tank is completely empty.

4. Joey seems to be sort of a slow reader.

5. There are very many reasons for the disparity in wealth among the world's nations.

6. Some experts believe that perhaps we are motivated simply by the desire to seek pleasure and to avoid pain.

7. In India, I found about the best food I have ever eaten.

8. She is a fairly excellent pianist.

9. The Hermitage Museum in St. Petersburg is filled with unique, one-of-a-kind paintings.

10. Needless to say, auditors should remain independent of the companies that they audit.

EXERCISE 3

Rewrite the following sentences, cutting out needless self-reference. Suggested answers are found on pages 119–120.

1. The speaker, in my personal opinion, is lost in details.

2. I feel, as many others do, that we ought to pay teachers as much as other professionals, such as doctors, lawyers, and engineers.

3. I do not think this argument can be generalized to those countries that have poor infrastructures.

4. My own experience shows me that wine is a fine social lubricant.

5. I'm really wondering whether more people would use the library if books and movies could be delivered to a person's home for a small fee.

6. Although I am no expert, I do not think that freedom of speech means that someone can scream "fire" in a crowded movie theatre and be held blameless.

7. If I had to venture a guess, I'd say that many individuals want to lose weight, but many fail simply because they do not decide on a diet program and then follow it diligently.

8. I must emphasize that I am not saying that the opposing argument is without merit.

9. If I were ever asked about the people that I find most inspiring, I would say that they are those individuals who are incredibly driven but incredibly humble.

10. It is my belief that to succeed in a relationship a person must be willing to give 70 percent and only expect to receive 30 percent.

# Principle 11

## Gain Active Power

☞ **Principle #11:**     **Favor active sentences, not passive sentences.**

In general, favor the active voice over the passive voice because the active voice is more action-oriented. The active voice is both more direct and less verbose, cutting down on the number of needed words. For example, the sentence "Harry loved Sally" is written in the active voice and contains three words. The sentence "Sally was loved by Harry" is written in the passive voice and contains five words.

In a normal Subject-Verb-Object sentence, the doer of the action appears at the front of the sentence and the receiver of the action appears at the end of the sentence. Passive sentences are less direct because they reverse the normal Subject-Verb-Object sentence order, placing the doer of the action at the end of the sentence and the receiver of the action at the front of the sentence.

Passive     *The company party was organized by the secretary.*

Active      *The secretary organized the company party.*

Passive sentences may also fail to mention the doer of the action.

Passive     *The writing of the report was easy.*

Active      *She wrote the report easily.*

Writing students are so often told to avoid the passive voice that it is not hard to understand why the mere mention of the passive voice leads some zealots to blurt out "passive bad, active good." It is not categorically correct to say that we should always avoid the passive voice. Sometimes, the passive voice is effective or even necessary. Such is the case when the writer must decide whether to expose or hide the identity of the doer of the action.

EXAMPLE 1

Passive     *Today, the computer files were erased.*
            (The writer's goal is to hide the perpetrator.)

Active      *Today, Calamity Jane erased the computer files.*
            (The writer's goal is to expose the perpetrator.)

EXAMPLE 2

Another reason for using the passive voice is variety.

*We sat through the visiting professor's intriguing lecture. The discussion centered on why people with higher I.Q.'s and lower E.Q.'s usually end up working for people with higher E.Q.'s but lower I.Q.'s. Afterwards, student questions were entertained.*

The passive voice is appropriate when the performer of the action is unknown or unimportant. In the first example below, the extraction of oil is deemed important but the extractor is not. In the second example, the discovery of the pearl is important but the discoverer is either unknown or deemed unimportant.

EXAMPLES 3 & 4

*Millions of barrels of oil were pumped from under the desert sand.*

*The world's largest pearl (6.4 kg) was discovered in the Philippines in 1934.*

Finally, the passive voice is likely preferred when the receiver of the action is more important than the performer of the action.

EXAMPLE 5

*Joyce Buckingham was awarded a medal by the committee organizers.*

> When imagining the passive voice, picture a young George Washington, hiding a hatchet behind his back, as he says to his father, "I cannot tell a lie: the cherry tree was chopped down."

EXERCISE

Rewrite the following sentences, replacing the passive voice with the active voice. Suggested answers are found on pages 120–121.

1.  In premodern times, medical surgery was often performed by inexperienced and ill-equipped practitioners.

2.  The main point made by the author can be found in the last paragraph.

3.  Motivational courses are often attended by those who need them least, while they are not sought out by those who have greatest need.

4.  The barbecue pits must be relocated where they can be used by campers.

5.  Details of the peace agreement were ironed out minutes before the deadline.

6.  Red Cross volunteers should be generously praised for their efforts.

7.  Actor agreements will always be negotiated by an actor's agent before being signed by the actor.

8.  Test results were posted with no concern for confidentiality.

9.  The report was compiled by a number of clinical psychologists and marriage experts.

10. Without money, staff, and local government support, many diseases in less developed countries cannot be treated.

# Principle 12

## Favor Verbs, Not Nouns

☞ **Principle #12:** **Avoid nominalizing your verbs and adjectives.**

The word nominalization is a fancy sounding but important concept in writing. It describes the process by which verbs and adjectives are turned into nouns. Nominalizations weaken writing for a variety of reasons, mainly because they make sentences longer and force the reader to work harder to extract the sentence's meaning. The next page shows several examples of nominalizations.

Avoid turning verbs into nouns:

| VERBS | NOUNS |
|---|---|
| *reduce* | *reduction* |
| *develop* | *development* |
| *rely* | *reliability* |

So, "reduction of costs" is best written as "reduce costs," "development of a 5-year plan" is best written as "develop a 5-year plan," and "reliability of the data" is best written as "rely on the data."

Avoid turning adjectives into nouns:

| ADJECTIVES | NOUNS |
|---|---|
| *precise* | *precision* |
| *creative* | *creativity* |
| *reasonable* | *reasonableness* |

So, "precision of measurements" is best written as "precise measurements," "creativity of individuals" is best written as "creative individuals," and "reasonableness of working hours" is best written as "reasonable working hours."

Also, all verbs can be turned into nouns (called gerunds) when adding *-ing* (for example, speaking, carrying, and engaging).

EXAMPLE

Original     *Is the drinking of alcohol by students allowed on campus?*

Better       *May students drink alcohol on campus?*

The gerund "drinking" is best changed to the verb "drink."

## EXERCISE

Rewrite the following sentences replacing nouns with either adjectives or verbs. Suggested answers are found on page 121.

1. Amateur cyclists must work on the development of their own training programs.

2. The inability to make decisions is a military leader's darkest enemy.

3. The expert panel's best estimate includes a 20 percent reduction in pollution as a result of the implementation of the new clean air bill.

4. Most dietitians advocate cutting down on the eating of fatty foods and reducing the intake of carbohydrates as the best means of losing weight.

5. Reasonableness and evenhandedness were not among the politician's strong suits.

6. The standardization of entrance exams helps ensure that students can apply to college and graduate school programs on an equal footing.

7. Hearing celebrities airing their political views on television should not be viewed as done in bad taste.

8. The applicability of using traditional accounting formulas for the valuation of Internet companies was never seriously questioned by investors prior to the first dot-com bust.

9. Our supervisor made a decision in favor of firing three employees.

10. Individuals who exhibit creativity and spontaneity should be encouraged to follow their dreams.

# Principle 13

## Use Parallel Forms

👉 **Principle #13:**  **Express a series of items in consistent, parallel form.**

Parallelism in writing means that we should express similar parts of a sentence in a consistent way. Elements alike in function should be alike in construction. Parallelism builds clarity and power. Note the following sentence in parallel form: "The high school entrepreneur created, financed, and marketed the new miracle tool." Now compare this with a nonparallel form: "The high school entrepreneur was involved in the creation of a new miracle tool, secured financing for it, and spent time getting the product to market."

Consider the parallelism in the famous quote by former U.S. President John F. Kennedy:

*Let every nation know, whether it wishes us well or ill, that we shall pay any price, bear any burden, meet any hardship, support any friend, oppose any foe to assure the survival and success of liberty.*

Note how all the verbs are in parallel form. Also, ponder the parallelism of this famous spiritual verse.

*Blessed are the poor in spirit: for theirs is the kingdom of heaven. Blessed are they that mourn: for they shall be comforted. Blessed are the meek: for they shall inherit the earth. Blessed are they which do hunger and thirst after righteousness: for they shall be filled.*

Parallelism may involve any part of speech, but especially verbs, prepositions, and conjunctions. They may also involve the articles *a, an,* and *the.*

Parallelism must be observed closely when we list a series of items. The rule here is that either we repeat the word before every element in a series or include it only before the first item. Anything else violates the rules of parallelism governing a series of items. Your treatment of the second element of the series determines the form of all subsequent elements.

EXAMPLE 1

Original       *Miguel went to Chile, Peru, and to Ecuador.*

Correct        *Miguel went to Chile, to Peru, and to Ecuador.*

Correct        *Miguel went to Chile, Peru, and Ecuador.*

EXAMPLE 2

Original       *She likes sun, sand, and going to the sea.*

Correct        *She likes the sun, the sand, and the sea.*

Correct        *She likes the sun, sand, and sea.*

EXAMPLE 3

Original       *The prime minister had met with military personnel,
               listened to his closest advisors, and had studied a recent
               poll result before deciding on military action.*

Correct        *The prime minister had met with military personnel,
               had listened to his closest advisors, and had studied a
               recent poll result before deciding on military action.*

Correct        *The prime minister had met with military personnel,
               listened to his closest advisors, and studied a recent poll
               result before deciding on military action.*

EXERCISE 1

Rewrite the following sentences using parallel structure.
Suggested answers appear on page 122.

1.  Despite winning the lottery, the elderly couple said they
    planned to spend money only on a new tractor, new stove,
    and a new porch.

2.  Olympic volunteers were ready, fully able, and were quite
    determined to do a great job.

3.  The documentary was interesting and replete with
    pertinent information.

4.  Wayne Gretsky was well-liked by his teammates and
    National Hockey League fans respected him.

5.  Students can log onto Facebook, spend time reading email
    messages, review some blog posts, and then tweet with joy.

6. The fund manager based his theory on stock performance, bond performance, and on other leading economic indicators.

7. The dancer taught her understudy how to move, to dress, how to work with choreographers and deal with photographers.

8. Just as the sound advice of a good lawyer can help win a court case so too can a sports match be won by the sound advice of a good coach.

9. According to the Buddhist mantra, fearfulness, feelings of anger, and needless desire lead to suffering. Eliminate fearfulness, feelings of anger, and needless desire and you eliminate suffering.

10. My objections regarding the pending impeachment are, first, the personal nature of the matter; second, that it is partisan.

## ELLIPTICAL EXPRESSIONS

Parallelism also involves rules for when we can acceptably eliminate words in a sentence and still retain clear meaning. Three potentially tricky situations may arise when using verbs, prepositions, and correlative conjunctions. In the case of verbs (or verb forms) and prepositions, it is okay to omit a second verb or preposition if it is the same as the first. To check for faulty parallelism, complete each component idea in a sentence and make sure each part of the sentence can stand alone. For instance, in the sentence "The speech was informative and funny," there is no need to say "The speech was informative and was funny," since the second verb "was" is the same as the first, and need not be written out.

## Verbs

Original    *In my favorite Japanese restaurant, the sushi is excellent and the drinks expensive.*

Correct    *In my favorite Japanese restaurant, the sushi is excellent and the drinks are expensive.*

*Definition* ∝ The verb in the second part of the sentence is different from the verb used in the first part of the sentence and must be written out.

## Prepositions

Original    *John is interested but not very good at golf.*

Correct    *John is interested in but not very good at golf.*

*Definition* ∝ The preposition in the second part of the sentence is different from the preposition used in the first part of the sentence and must be written out.

## Correlative Conjunctions

Correlative conjunctions include "either ... or," "neither ... nor," "not only ... but also," and "both ... and." If a verb is placed before the first component part in the correlative construction, then the verb need not be repeated. If the verb is placed after the first component part in the correlative construction, then it must be placed after the second item as well.

Original    *She not only likes beach volleyball but also snow skiing.*

Correct    *She likes not only beach volleyball but also snow skiing.*

Correct    *She not only likes beach volleyball but also likes snow skiing.*

*NOTE* ∽ The first correct version above is arguably more popular.

EXERCISE 2

Rewrite the following sentences using parallel structure.
Suggested answers are found on pages 123–124.

1.  The painting may be done either with watercolors or oils.

2.  Tasmania has and always will be an island.

3.  Who is not interested and astounded by this fact?—A
    million seconds ago was 11.5 days ago; a billion seconds
    ago was 31 years ago; a trillion seconds ago was 310
    centuries ago or 31 millennia ago!

4.  Massage creates a relaxing, therapeutic, and rejuvenating
    experience both for your body and your well-being.

5.  Samantha is intrigued but not very proficient at
    handwriting analysis.

6.  A good scientist not only thinks logically but also creatively.

7.  Brian will not ask nor listen to any advice.

8.  Either we forget our plans or accept their proposal.

9.  A dilemma facing many young professionals is whether to
    choose to work for money or to work for enjoyment.

10. Neither should one lie to good friends nor be so
    patronizing as to not tell them the truth.

> Writing is part science and part art. That writing
> be structured and conform to rules is science.
> That writing may vary with each situation is art.

# Principle 14

## Capitalize on Sentence Variety

☞ Principle #14:     Vary the length and beginnings of your sentences.

The normal sentence pattern in English is subject-verb-object (S-V-O), as seen in the example "I play tennis." Most sentences should follow this subject-verb-object sequence because it produces the most power. However, if all sentences follow this order, our writing becomes choppy and monotonous. Particularly noticeable are series of sentences all beginning the same way, especially with "I" or "we." Here are ten ways to vary sentence beginnings.

## WITH A SUBJECT

*Customers* can tell us why products sell if we take the time to listen to them.

*Definition* ○₰ The subject is what or whom the sentence is about.

## WITH A PHRASE

*For this reason,* no product is to be built until we know a market exists for it.

*Definition* ○₰ A phrase is a group of words that does not contain a verb.

## WITH A CLAUSE

*Because human beings are complex,* the sales process cannot be reduced to a simple formula.

*Definition* ○₰ A clause is a group of words that does contain a verb.

## WITH AN ARTICLE

*A* good batting average is an arguably more important statistic in baseball than is the number of home runs achieved.

*Definition* ○₰ There are three articles in English—*a, an,* and *the.*

## WITH A VERB

*Try* not to text during the speech.

*Definition* ○₰ A verb is a word that expresses an action or a state of being.

## WITH AN ADVERB

*Understandably,* students like to hear entrepreneurs speak of rags-to-riches stories.

*Definition* ℘ An adverb is a word that modifies a verb, an adjective, or another adverb. When adverbs are used to begin sentences (usually followed by a comma), they can be referred to as "opening sentence" adverbs.

## WITH ADJECTIVES

<u>Intelligent</u> and <u>compassionate</u>, *Dorothy has the ingredients to be a leader.*

*Definition* ℘ An adjective is a word used to modify or describe a noun or pronoun.

## WITH A GERUND

<u>Traveling</u> *to a country is more meaningful when you first invest time reading about its geography and history.*

*Definition* ℘ A gerund is a noun formed with -*ing*. Informally it is said to be "a noun that looks like a verb."

## WITH AN INFINITIVE

<u>To be a monk</u>, *a person must be able to relinquish selfishness in order to concentrate on a higher goal.*

*Definition* ℘ An infinitive is a noun that is formed by a verb preceded by *to*.

## WITH CORRELATIVE CONJUNCTIONS

<u>Not only</u> *poverty* <u>but also</u> *pollution threatens the development of the third world.*

*Definition* ℘ A conjunction is a word that joins or connects words, phrases, clauses, or sentences. A correlative conjunction joins parts of a sentence that are of equal weight. Four common correlative conjunctions include "either ... or," "neither ... nor," "not only ... but (also)," and "both ... and."

Exercise

*Selling is difficult. It requires practical experience and personal initiative.*

To practice this principle, rearrange the above sentence to satisfy the different headings below. You may have to change the content of the sentence for the purpose of this exercise. Suggested answers appear on pages 124–125.

1. With a Subject

2. With a Phrase

3. With a Clause

4. With an Article

5. With a Verb

6. With an Adverb

7. With Adjectives

8. With a Gerund

9. With an Infinitive

10. With Correlative Conjunctions

# Principle 15

## Choose an Appropriate Tone

👉 **Principle #15:    Write with a positive, personal tone.**

Tone is a difficult thing to describe; some define it as the writer's attitude. Tone occurs along two major dimensions: positive or negative and formal or informal. Today, a positive and personal tone is appropriate on most writing occasions. One way to control writing tone is through your choice of positive versus negative words. Use positive words whenever possible; readers instinctively dislike being told what is not true as opposed to what is true. Thus, even negative forms can be turned into positive expressions.

## POSITIVE VS. NEGATIVE TONE

Negative      *The store will close at 7 p.m.*

*NOTE* ∽ This uses a negative verb "close."

Positive      *The store will remain open until 7 p.m.*

*NOTE* ∽ This uses a positive adjective "open."

Negative      *The plan is not sound.*

*NOTE* ∽ This uses a negative word; it tells us what isn't true as opposed to what is true.

Positive      *The plan has drawbacks.*

*NOTE* ∽ This states deficiencies in a positive manner; it tells us what is true.

## FORMAL VS. INFORMAL TONE

Writing may have a formal or an informal tone. Two factors that influence formality are the use of contractions and personal pronouns.

### Use of Personal Pronouns

Add personal pronouns to make your writing more informal and personable.

No pronouns      *Please send any follow-up questions to the customer service department.*

Pronouns      *If you have any follow-up questions, please contact our customer service department.*

No pronouns          *The Chief Executive Officer is aware that*
                     *strengthening product quality is the key to turning*
                     *around the company.*

Pronouns             *Our Chief Executive Officer believes that we need*
                     *to strengthen product quality in order to turn the*
                     *company around.*

A complete list of personal pronouns include:

1st person           *I, me, my, mine, we, us, ours*

2nd person           *you, your, yours*

3rd person           *he, she, they, him, her, them, it, his, hers, its, their,*
                     *theirs*

Also                 *who, whom, whose*

## Use of Contractions

Add contractions (for example, *can't, isn't, shouldn't, won't*) if you
want your writing to come across as informal.

No contractions          *The stockholders have not voted on a new*
                         *Chief Executive Officer.*

Contractions             *The stockholders haven't voted on a new*
                         *Chief Executive Officer.*

Other factors also affect whether a document is considered
formal, informal, or semi-formal (see following page). A personal
letter or e-mail is typically informal, while a business report is
formal. A business letter is a good example of a semi-formal
document: It usually contains informal characteristics (for
example, use of contractions, first-person pronouns, colloquial
expressions, and simple or non-technical vocabulary) as well
as formal characteristics (for example, formal salutations and
signatures).

## CHARTING THE FORMAL AND INFORMAL TONES

The two "pyramids" below highlight the characteristics of a formal and informal tone.

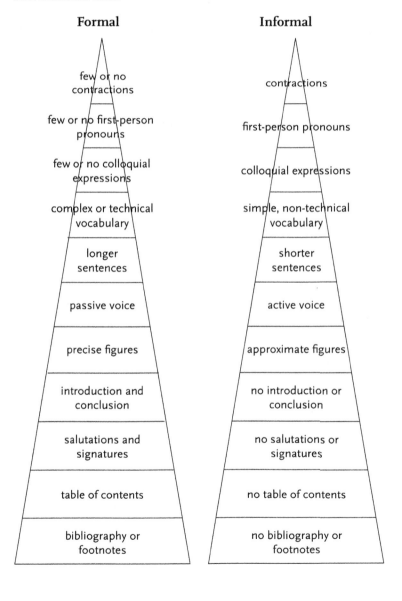

| Formal | Informal |
|---|---|
| few or no contractions | contractions |
| few or no first-person pronouns | first-person pronouns |
| few or no colloquial expressions | colloquial expressions |
| complex or technical vocabulary | simple, non-technical vocabulary |
| longer sentences | shorter sentences |
| passive voice | active voice |
| precise figures | approximate figures |
| introduction and conclusion | no introduction or conclusion |
| salutations and signatures | no salutations or signatures |
| table of contents | no table of contents |
| bibliography or footnotes | no bibliography or footnotes |

NOTE ✍ Although the use contractions is now widespread, there are two theories on the effect of their use. The first theory or majority view is to use contractions because they reinforce a personal tone. The second or minority view is that although contractions are fine for use in writing e-mails and personal letters, it is preferable to avoid them in formal documents such as essays and reports.

<u>EXERCISE</u>

Make this letter "warmer" by using a more positive and personal tone. This is a semi-formal document, and it is recommended that contractions not be used. A suggested revision is found on page 125.

---

Dear Mr. Jones:

Comptronics Inc. deeply regrets the problems experienced with your notebook computer, Model 580G. The company's engineers examined the unit and decided that the problems were so massive that they were not able to make repairs. The two remaining options are either to take a refund on the unit, or to request replacement with a new model. Please inform the service department of a decision, and Comptronics Inc. will quickly respond.

Sincerely,

*Mr. Do Good*
Service Representative
Comptronics Inc.

---

Tone is attitude. A formal tone is like formal attire that keeps distance between the writer and reader. Most writing favors an informal tone.

# Principle 16

## Keep Your Writing Gender Neutral

☞ **Principle #16:** **Avoid using the masculine generic to refer to both genders.**

The masculine generic refers to the sole use of the pronoun "he" or "him" when referring to situations involving both genders. Avoid using "he" when referring to either a he or a she; likewise, avoid using "him" when referring to either a him or a her. Be sensitive in acknowledging both sexes. Because 50 percent of any general readership is likely female, it is not only politically astute but fair-minded to avoid using the masculine generic.

Consider the following sentences from a female perspective.

ORIGINAL

*Today's chief executive must be extremely well rounded. He must be not only corporate and civic minded but also environmentally focused and entrepreneurially spirited.*

There are essentially two ways to remedy this. Replace "he" with "he or she," or recast the sentence in the plural, using "they" or "them."

BETTER

*Today's chief executive must be extremely well rounded. He or she must be not only corporate and civic minded but also environmentally focused and entrepreneurially spirited.*

EQUALLY PROPER

*Today's chief executives must be extremely well rounded. They must be not only corporate and civic minded but also environmentally focused and entrepreneurially spirited.*

A final way to address the problem, especially when writing longer documents, is to alternate between the use of "he" and "she." The disadvantage in this approach, however, is that the arbitrary, alternate use of these two pronouns may annoy the reader and cause confusion.

We must also watch for and replace words that represent the masculine generic. Here is a partial list:

| MASCULINE GENERIC | BETTER |
|---|---|
| *ad man* | *advertising executive* |
| *anchorman* | *anchor* |
| *chairman* | *chair, chairperson* |
| *Englishmen* | *the English* |
| *fireman* | *firefighter* |
| *man-hours* | *work-hours, person-hours* |
| *mankind* | *humans, humankind, humanity* |
| *policeman* | *police officer* |
| *postman, mailman* | *mail carrier, postal agent* |
| *salesman* | *salesperson, sales representative* |
| *self-made man* | *self-made person* |
| *businessman* | *businessperson* |
| *congressman* | *member of Congress,* |
| | *Senator, Representative* |
| *spokesman* | *spokesperson* |
| *landlord* | *land owner* |
| *layman* | *layperson* |
| *man-made* | *synthetic, artificial* |
| *workman* | *worker* |

It is sometimes necessary to replace the feminine generic:

| FEMININE GENERIC | BETTER |
|---|---|
| *housewife* | *homemaker* |
| *maid/cleaning lady* | *domestic, housekeeper* |
| *maiden name* | *birth name, former name* |
| *secretary (office)* | *office assistant* |
| *stewardess* | *flight attendant* |

# Part III

# Readability

*Put it before them briefly
so they will read it, clearly so they
will appreciate it, picturesquely so
they will remember it and, above
all, accurately, so they will be
guided by its light.*

—Joseph Pulitzer

# Principle 17

## Capitalize on Layout and Design

☞ Principle #17:    Add more space around your writing to increase readability.

The easiest way to make writing more readable is to increase your document's margin. Also, ensuring that a blank line separates paragraphs will let your composition breathe. Avoid writing one big block of words pressed tight against the edges of the page. Two versions of an identical document appear on the next two pages; the second is easier to read simply because it employs more space in the margins and between paragraphs.

## ORIGINAL VERSION

### Paradox of Our Time by Dr. Bob Moorehead

The paradox of our time in history is that we have taller buildings but shorter tempers, wider freeways, but narrower viewpoints. We spend more, but have less; we buy more, but enjoy less. We have bigger houses and smaller families, more conveniences, but less time. We have more degrees but less sense, more knowledge, but less judgment, more experts, yet more problems, more medicine, but less wellness.

We drink too much, smoke too much, spend too recklessly, laugh too little, drive too fast, get angry too quickly, stay up too late, get up too tired, read too little, watch TV too much, and pray too seldom.

We have multiplied our possessions, but reduced our values. We talk too much, love too seldom, and hate too often.

We've learned how to make a living, but not a life. We've added years to life, not life to years. We've been all the way to the moon and back, but have trouble crossing the street to meet a new neighbor. We conquered outer space, but not inner space. We've done larger things, but not better things.

We've cleaned up the air, but polluted the soul. We've conquered the atom, but not our prejudice. We write more, but learn less. We plan more, but accomplish less. We've learned to rush, but not to wait. We build more computers to hold more information, to produce more copies than ever, but we communicate less and less.

These are times of fast foods and slow digestion, of tall men and short character, of steep profits and shallow relationships. These are the days of two incomes but more divorce, of fancier houses, but broken homes. These are days of quick trips, disposable diapers, throwaway morality, overweight bodies, and pills that do everything from cheer, to quiet, to kill. It is a time when there is much in the showroom window and nothing in the stockroom.

IMPROVED VERSION

### Paradox of Our Time by Dr. Bob Moorehead

The paradox of our time in history is that we have taller buildings but shorter tempers, wider freeways, but narrower viewpoints. We spend more, but have less; we buy more, but enjoy less. We have bigger houses and smaller families, more conveniences, but less time. We have more degrees but less sense, more knowledge, but less judgment, more experts, yet more problems, more medicine, but less wellness.

We drink too much, smoke too much, spend too recklessly, laugh too little, drive too fast, get angry too quickly, stay up too late, get up too tired, read too little, watch TV too much, and pray too seldom.

We have multiplied our possessions, but reduced our values. We talk too much, love too seldom, and hate too often.

We've learned how to make a living, but not a life. We've added years to life, not life to years. We've been all the way to the moon and back, but have trouble crossing the street to meet a new neighbor. We conquered outer space, but not inner space. We've done larger things, but not better things.

We've cleaned up the air, but polluted the soul. We've conquered the atom, but not our prejudice. We write more, but learn less. We plan more, but accomplish less. We've learned to rush, but not to wait. We build more computers to hold more information, to produce more copies than ever, but we communicate less and less.

These are times of fast foods and slow digestion, of tall men and short character, of steep profits and shallow relationships. These are the days of two incomes but more divorce, of fancier houses, but broken homes. These are days of quick trips, disposable diapers, throwaway morality, overweight bodies, and pills that do everything from cheer, to quiet, to kill. It is a time when there is much in the showroom window and nothing in the stockroom.

# Principle 18

## Employ Readability Tools

☞ **Principle #18:** **Make key words and phrases stand out.**

Painters, sculptors, musicians, professional photographers, and poets are but a few individuals highly adept at judging what effect stylistic additions and deductions will have on an overall composition. Writing is also a balancing act. The writer seeks to retain those greater elements that most define a writing piece while looking for smaller adornments to bolster its appearance and readability. In the writing arena, such adornments might include boldface type, italics, dashes, bullets, enumerations, and shading.

## BOLDS

Bolds (boldface type) may be used to emphasize keywords and help key ideas "jump out" at the reader. Bolds are especially useful for flyers, résumés, and other documents in which the reader may spend only a brief time reviewing. Italics or underlining can do the same job as bold type, though care must be exercised not to overdo it. For example, rarely do we want to see bolds and italics used in the same paragraph. One unwritten rule of writing and editing is to never use bolds, italics, and underlines together (ditto for bolds, italics, and full caps in combination). Be aware that if you use boldface type too liberally, you will dull the effect and perhaps patronize the reader.

## ITALICS

There is artistry in the occasional use of italics. Italics, like bolds, serve similar purposes. Consider using italics to highlight certain key words, especially those that show contrast, or for small words, especially negative words such as *not, no,* and *but.* Be careful of overusing italics because they are tiring on the eye and can make the page look busy.

For stylistic purposes, many examples in this book appear in italics in order to distinguish them from explanatory text. Note that such text would not normally be italicized.

## DASHES

Dashes can be used to vary the rhythm of a sentence and to place emphasis on words and phrases in a more dynamic manner than could be achieved through the use of a comma (or pair of commas) or semicolon.

*The world's oldest dated book—the Diamond Sutra—is an elaborately decorated book containing a beautiful cover piece. Written in 868 A.D., it was discovered in 1907 in a cave near Dunhuang, China.*

Note how the dashes in the previous example make the reference to the book appear more dramatic than in the example below, which contains commas:

*The world's oldest dated book, the Diamond Sutra, is an elaborately decorated book containing a beautiful cover piece. Written in 868 A.D., it was discovered in 1907 in a cave near Dunhuang, China.*

## BULLETS

Bullets (•) are effective tools for paraphrasing information, especially for presenting information in short phrases when formal sentences are not required. Bullets are most commonly used when preparing résumés, slides, or flyers. Bullets are not, however, recommended for use in the main body of an essay or report unless they are included within a table. It is also not considered good practice in formal writing to use hyphens (-) or asterisks (*) in place of bullets.

## ENUMERATIONS

Enumerations involve the numbering of points. Listing items by number is more formal but very useful for ordering ideas or data.

## EXAMPLE 1

*I feel that my greatest long-term contributions working in this field will be measured by (1) my ability to find ways to define and quantify, in dollars and cents, the benefits of ethics and corporate citizenship, and (2) my ability to sell corporations on the proactive benefits of these programs as a means to market their company, products, and employees.*

## EXAMPLE 2

*Each letter in the word "s.u.c.c.e.s.s." embodies a single action:*

1. *Super effort*
2. *Unusual drive*
3. *Copy what works.*
4. *Change what doesn't.*
5. *Exercise now and cut out excess.*
6. *Save a little more, spend a little less.*
7. *Start all over again the very next day.*

SHADING

Shading creates contrast on the page and can be a great device for formatting business reports. For example, you can highlight the start of each section of a report by using shaded section headings. Within the pages of a report, shading is often used to tint the top row (header row) of a table. Flyers also commonly use shading to call out information.

RÉSUMÉ EXAMPLE

The following is an excerpt from a résumé. Résumés provide a classic example of the use of readability tools, particularly in terms of bullets, bolds, and italics.

---

*PROFESSIONAL EXPERIENCE*

2012–present     **BANK OF AMERICA**, Hartford, Conn.
*Financial Analyst*
- Analyzed branch performance and devised new strategies to improve regional market share. Formulated a two-year marketing plan for two branches.
- Developed a new commission system and assisted in its implementation.
- Presented tax saving strategies and advice on investment portfolio compositions for principal clients.

# Principle 19

## Use Headings and Headlines

☞ Principle #19:   Use headings and headlines to divide or summarize your writing.

Because organization is particularly important in academic writing, which tends to be longer, and because time and money are of critical importance in business, both headings and headlines help convey information efficiently. Headlines are similar to headings; the difference lies in their length and purpose. Headings are usually a couple of words in length; headlines are usually a line or two in length. The purpose of headings is to divide information under sections; the primary purpose of headlines is to summarize or paraphrase information that follows.

## EFFECTIVE USE OF HEADINGS

With the use of headings in the document below, the writer is able to direct the reader's attention; without headings, the reader would have a harder job of accessing the information efficiently.

---

### The Four Cs

**Color**
The most desirable diamonds are colorless. The color scale starts at D and descends through Z. Although the best color is D (colorless), diamonds also come in a range of natural fancy tones, such as blue, pink, green, and red. Believe it or not, these fancy diamonds are particularly rare, and like their colorless counterparts, can also fetch a high price tag.

**Clarity**
Gemologists refer to imperfections in diamond clarity as "inclusions"; the fewer inclusions, the more valuable the stone.

**Cut**
What makes a diamond stand out beyond any other precious gemstone? Certainly the way it sparkles. While nature determines the color and clarity of a stone, diamond cut is solely dependent upon the skill of the cutter.

**Carat Weight**
The word carat comes from the carob seeds that were used to balance scales in ancient times. Carat therefore refers to size. It is not necessarily true that the larger the carat, the more valuable the diamond. The value of a stone will always be a combination of the four Cs: color, clarity, cut, and carat size.

---

## EFFECTIVE USE OF HEADLINES

Headlines are effective tools in summarizing complete sections of a business report or personal essay. The headlines below appear in italics.

---

### The Land, Sea, and Sky Must Guide Me

The land, the sky, and the sea: These three environments and the experiences they have given me have influenced and helped shape who I am today.

*When I go back to the land in the northern part of Denmark, I walk across the fields and hear the birds singing.*

The land has taught me to appreciate my base and family stability. _____ _____ _____.

*The smallest corals in bright colors can be poisonous, while the sharks may be friendly.*

When scuba diving, I have learned to expect the unexpected. _____ _____ _____.

*The sky is a reminder that many things are possible even though they seem beyond our reach.*

Sky diving has encouraged me to stretch and reach new heights. _____ _____ _____.

One of the big challenges I am meeting in life is the challenge of being successful in both my personal and career life. In meeting these challenges, all of my influences must guide me – the land, the sea, and the sky.

# Principle 20

## Go Back and Rework Your Writing

☞ Principle #20:  Wait until your writing stands still before you call it finished.

Rare is the writer who can sit down and knock out a perfect writing draft without corrections. Most proficient writers take at least three drafts to finish short pieces of writing. For example, you may be writing a cover letter to accompany your updated résumé. First, you write to get your ideas down on paper. Second, you edit through what you have written, add detail, make connections, and make corrections. Third, you wait twenty-four hours and reread, making minor changes. The longer the work, the more times this process is repeated for individual sections.

The number of drafts required for an entire work depends on the work's length and complexity. A two-line office memo is likely to be done in a single draft because it is short and simple. A one-page poem might take more than a dozen drafts because it is longer and more difficult.

## WHEN IS IT REALLY FINISHED?

Making changes to your writing is annoying and grueling. But eventually, with changes made, you will likely be satisfied with what you have written and not want to add or delete anything. This is the point at which your writing is finished—your writing is "standing still." Unpolished writing is like shifting sand in a desert storm. Eventually the storm ceases, and the sand sits still. The word "finished," when referring to writing, should really be enclosed in quotation marks because writing is never actually finished. With respect to writing done for everyday purposes, completion is an end in itself. However, for more permanent written works, such as novels, writing can be continued indefinitely because it can always be improved. Even published books can be reworked and reedited. Weeks, months, and years after a book is published, an author will invariably contemplate changes.

## APPRECIATE THE PROCESS

Writing is a creative process. You discover things as you force yourself to write. What is especially satisfying is turning "junk" writing into something worthwhile. When you put together a lengthy piece, such as a personal essay or business report, you will naturally begin by writing some areas well. Other areas you'll not be satisfied with, and those must be reworked.

Let's call the parts you like "flowers" and the parts you dislike "dirt." As you focus your efforts on the "dirt," you begin to make improvements, and sometimes to your surprise, these areas become as good as, or better than, one or more of the "flowers." This is extremely satisfying. You are inspired. You gain energy.

You now try to improve other "dirt" areas until there are none left. Later, you go back to an original "flowered" area and make it even better, thus raising it up one notch from anything done before. The writing process is a ongoing process of producing flowers and dirt.

Most people hate reworking their writing. It is human nature. The pressure and agony of writing is one reason why alcohol has been humorously dubbed "the occupational hazard of professional writers." It is not writing per se, but the rewriting and redrafting process that can drive a person to drink. Worse is the reality of knowing that even before you begin to write—no matter how well you write—your writing will require revision. Fortunately, for most students and business professionals, the everyday writing process is not filled with the same emotional highs and lows as it is for a person who makes a living from writing.

It is a great feeling to look at something you wrote a long time ago, be it an old college essay, business report, personal letter, or poem, and say to yourself, "Wow, this is funny. Some of this stuff blows me away! How did I come up with it?" There is no absolute answer. Skill, luck, boldness, and naiveté are key ingredients in the writing process.

PRINCIPLE 3 (Page 27)

The most probable solution to the whale essay is to organize the sentences in the following order: 5, 2, 1, 4, 3.

THE WHALE

*The whale is the largest mammal in the animal kingdom. When most people think of whales, they think of sluggish, obese animals, frolicking freely in the ocean and eating tons of food to sustain themselves. When people think of ants, on the other hand, they tend to think of hardworking underfed creatures transporting objects twice their body size to and from hidden hideaways. However, if we analyze food consumption based on body size, we find that ants eat their full body weight every day, while a whale eats the equivalent of only one-thousandth of its body weight each day. In fact, when we compare the proportionate food consumption of all living creatures, we find that the whale is one the most food-efficient creatures on earth.*

*NOTE* ❧ In the above paragraph, the conclusion appears in the last line. If a writing piece is very short and uncomplicated, there is little harm in putting the conclusion at the end. This may seem like an exception to Principle 1, and it is, but it represents the art of writing as opposed to the science of writing.

PRINCIPLE 6 (Page 45)

1.  Joannie has a German Shepherd and a Siamese cat.

2.  The vacation cost nearly $5,000.

3.  Rainbows contain a full spectrum of colors, including red, orange, yellow, green, blue, indigo, and violet.

4.  Sheila is 5'10" tall and has an attractive, baby-shaped face.

5. Many economists think that the Federal Reserve Bank's failure to lower bank interest rates is the reason for the current economic downturn.

6. Firms should use billboard advertising because it is low-cost and can increase sales as much as 10 percent in a given region.

7. Tim often misplaces his car keys.

8. The contestant was eliminated in the first round because she couldn't remember that Antarctica is one of the seven continents.

9. Fresh produce, small cans, and large boxes line each row of the grocery store from floor to ceiling.

10. Mr. and Mrs. Jones spend most of their time together, often laughing at each other's jokes.

PRINCIPLE 7 (Page 59)

≈ A good idea is cool!
≈ A good idea stands out.
≈ A good idea may get a chilly reception.
≈ A good idea can easily disappear.
≈ A good idea sure seems natural.
≈ A good idea has a big effect on its surroundings.
≈ You have to go a long way to find a good idea.
≈ A good idea takes time to form.
≈ If you overlook a good idea, it can sink you.
≈ You only see part of a good idea because there is more to it than meets the eye.
≈ There is a lot of depth in a good idea, but not everyone appreciates it.
≈ One-tenth of the benefit of a good idea is clearly visible, but nine-tenths of the long-term benefits lie below the surface.

PRINCIPLE 8 (Page 62)

1.   Recent studies suggest that carrot juice is good for you.

2.   We expect to use hundreds of reams of recycled copy paper in the next 12 months.

3.   This plan will eliminate inefficient shipping practices.

4.   Our schoolchildren's education should emphasize the three Rs—reading, writing, and arithmetic.

5.   Only meteorologists can analyze changing climatic conditions.

6.   When the poet wrote the second and third stanzas, he must have felt despair. (Or: I feel despair when reading the poem's second and third stanzas.)

7.   That is a fine dog.

     Note that a follow-up sentence is likely required to supply more details as to what a fine dog is.

8.   The hurricane destroyed almost all structures along the coastline.

9.   While I am against war, I also realize that some situations require the use of military force.

10.  Like Napoleon's army that marched on Russia more than a century before, the German army was also unable to successfully invade Russia because its soldiers were inadequately prepared for winter conditions.

*NOTE* ✑ The last three examples above require cutting out sentences to achieve simplicity. Such sentences may repeat information that the reader has otherwise gleaned from sentences that come immediately before or after.

PRINCIPLE 10, EXERCISE 1 (Page 70)

1. Attendees should adhere to the event's formal dress code.

2. A construction project that large needs an effective manager.

3. The Acropolis Museum remains a significant tourist attraction.

4. The conclusion is that physical and psychological symptoms are intertwined.

5. The field superintendent's charisma does not mask his poor technical knowledge.

6. The recent trend of government borrowing may create poorer nations.

7. These events—water shortages, chronic overcrowding, and rampant disease—have combined to create a crisis.

8. Few people can find novel solutions to problems.

9. She has chosen to work for UNESCO.

10. Negotiation opens many doors to peaceful settlement.

PRINCIPLE 10, EXERCISE 2 (Page 71)

1. Peter is an exceptional student.

2. You are the best person to decide what you should do with your life.

3. The propane tank is empty.

4. Joey is a slow reader.

5. There are many reasons for the disparity of wealth among the world's nations.

6. Some experts believe that we are motivated simply by the desire to seek pleasure and to avoid pain.

7. In India, I found the best food I have ever eaten.

8. She is an excellent pianist.

9. The Hermitage Museum in St. Petersburg is filled with unique paintings.

10. Auditors should remain independent of the companies that they audit.

PRINCIPLE 10, EXERCISE 3 (Page 72)

1. The speaker is lost in details.

2. We ought to pay teachers as much as other professionals, such as doctors, lawyers, and engineers.

3. This argument cannot be generalized to those countries with poor infrastructures.

4. Wine is a fine social lubricant.

5. Would more people use the library if books and movies could be delivered to a person's home for a small charge?

6. Freedom of speech does not mean that someone can scream "fire" in a crowded movie theatre and be held blameless.

7. Many individuals want to lose weight, but many fail simply because they do not decide on a diet plan and then follow it diligently.

8.  I am not saying that the opposing argument is without merit. (Or: The argument has merit.)

9.  The most inspiring individuals are those who are incredibly driven but incredibly humble.

10. To succeed in a relationship, a person must be willing to give 70 percent and only expect to receive 30 percent.

PRINCIPLE 11 (Page 76)

1.  In premodern times, inexperienced and ill-equipped practitioners often performed medical surgery.

2.  The author makes the main point in the last paragraph.

3.  Those who attend motivational courses often need them least, while those who choose not to attend usually need them most.

4.  We must relocate the barbecue pits so campers can use them.

5.  Negotiators ironed out the details of the peace agreement minutes before the deadline.

6.  Citizens should generously praise Red Cross volunteers for their efforts.

7.  A talent agent always negotiates an actor's agreement before an actor signs it.

8.  The institute posted test results with no concern for confidentiality.

9.  A number of clinical psychologists and marriage experts compiled the report.

10. Without money, staff, and local government support, doctors cannot treat diseases in less developed countries.

*NOTE* ✍ In examples 5, 8, and 10 above, the suggested solutions involve supplying a subject (that is, *negotiators, institute, and doctors*).

PRINCIPLE 12 (Page 79)

1. Amateur cyclists must develop their own training programs.

2. A military leader who is unable to decide faces a dark enemy.

3. The expert panel estimates that the new clean air bill, when fully implemented, will reduce pollution by 20 percent.

4. According to most dietitians, the best way for dieters to achieve weight loss is to reduce their intakes of fatty foods and carbohydrates.

5. The politician was neither reasonable nor evenhanded.

6. Standardized entrance exams help ensure that students can apply to college and graduate school programs on an equal footing.

7. Celebrities should feel free to air their political views on television.

8. Prior to the first dot-com bust, investors never seriously questioned whether traditional accounting formulas should be used to value Internet companies.

9. Our supervisor decided to fire three employees.

10. Creative, spontaneous individuals should be encouraged to follow their dreams.

PRINCIPLE 13, EXERCISE 1 (Pages 82–83)

1. Despite winning the lottery, the elderly couple said they planned to spend money only on a new tractor, a new stove, and a new porch.

2. Olympic volunteers were ready, able, and determined to do a great job.

3. The documentary was interesting and informative.

4. Wayne Gretsky was well-liked by his teammates and respected by National Hockey League fans.

   If the subject, Wayne Gretsky, is understood, we could write: His teammates liked him and National Hockey League fans respected him.

5. Students can check Facebook, read email messages, review blog posts, and then joyfully send tweets.

6. The fund manager based his theory on stock performance, on bond performance, and on other leading economic indicators.

7. The dancer taught her understudy how to move, dress, work with choreographers, and deal with photographers.

8. Just as the sound advice of a good lawyer can help win a court case, so too can the sound advice of a good coach help win a sports match.

9. According to the Buddhist mantra, fear, anger, and desire lead to suffering. Eliminate fear, anger, and desire and you eliminate suffering.

10. My objections regarding the pending impeachment are, first, the personal nature of the matter; second, the partisan nature of the matter.

## PRINCIPLE 13, EXERCISE 2 (Page 85)

1.  The painting may be done either with watercolors or with oils.

    Or: The painting may be done with either watercolors or oils.

2.  Tasmania has been and always will be an island.

3.  Who is not interested in and astounded by this fact?—A million seconds ago was 11.5 days ago; a billion seconds ago was 31 years ago; and a trillion seconds ago was 310 centuries ago or 31 millennia ago!

4.  Massage creates a relaxing, therapeutic, and rejuvenating experience both for your body and for your well-being.

    Or: Massage creates a relaxing, therapeutic, and rejuvenating experience for both your body and your well-being.

5.  Samantha is intrigued with but not very proficient at handwriting analysis.

6.  A good scientist not only thinks logically but also thinks creatively.

    Or: A good scientist thinks not only logically but also creatively.

7.  Brian will not ask for or listen to any advice.

8.  We either forget our plans or accept their proposal.

    Or: Either we forget our plans or we accept their proposal.

9.  A dilemma facing many young professionals is whether to work for money or to work for enjoyment.

10. One should neither lie to good friends nor be so patronizing as to not tell them the truth.

    Or: Neither should one lie to good friends nor should one be so patronizing as to not tell them the truth.

PRINCIPLE 14 (Page 89)

1.  With a subject: <u>Selling</u> is difficult because it requires practical experience and personal initiative.

2.  With a phrase: <u>For many reasons,</u> selling is difficult.

3.  With a clause: <u>Because it requires both practical experience and personal initiative,</u> selling is difficult.

4.  With an article: <u>The</u> reason selling is difficult is that it requires both practical experience and personal initiative.

5.  With a verb: <u>Use</u> your experience and your instincts and you will succeed in a selling career.

6.  With an adverb: <u>Traditionally,</u> the terms "sales" and "marketing" were used interchangeably.

7.  With adjectives: <u>Confident</u> and <u>resourceful,</u> a salesperson must possess these two key traits.

8.  With a gerund: <u>Requiring</u> a person to have both practical experience and personal initiative, selling is difficult.

9.  With an infinitive: <u>To be</u> an effective salesperson, one must be able to accept disappointment and work in an unpredictable environment.

10. With correlative conjunctions: <u>Not only</u> practical experience <u>but also</u> personal initiative is required to be a good salesperson.

PRINCIPLE 15 (Page 94)

When making the letter more positive, eliminate negative words such as "not able" and "so massive." Also add personal pronouns such as "you" and "yours." Moreover, "our company" sounds better than "Comptronics"; "our service department" sounds better than "the service department." The original letter contains two personal pronouns, namely *your* and *they*; the letter below contains ten uses of personal pronouns, namely *our, your, you, our, you, you, us, your, our,* and *your*.

---

Dear Mr. Jones:

Our company deeply regrets hearing of the problems you experienced with your notebook computer, Model 580G. Our engineers have examined the unit and believe that the best solution involves one of two choices:

(1) You receive a full refund on the unit, or (2) you allow us to replace your computer with a new model.

Please let our service department know your decision.

Sincerely,

*Mr. Do Good*
Service Representative
Comptronics Inc.

---

# Part IV

# Grammar

Part IV

*It's not wise to violate
the rules until you know
how to observe them.*

—T.S. Eliot

# 100-Question Quiz

The following 100-question quiz (Q1 to Q100) provides a highly distilled review of grammar, diction, and idioms. The first segment of this quiz addresses grammar and is built on the "big six" grammar categories: subject-verb agreement, modification, pronoun usage, parallelism, comparisons, and verb tenses. The "big six" grammar categories provide a way to break grammar into those areas where errors are most likely to occur. Once we study the rules within each category, we can immediately apply them to many practical writing situations.

Answers to the 100-question quiz are found on pages 156–176. Many of the terms used in this section are defined in the following sections titled *Grammatical Munchkins* and *Word Gremlins*. These sections can be reviewed first, before attempting quiz questions, if a more technical grounding is desired. Special notes (marked by *NOTE* ✍) provide additional commentary as needed.

## Subject-Verb Agreement

The overarching principle regarding subject-verb agreement is that singular subjects require singular verbs while plural subjects take plural verbs. Our objective is to identify the subject in order to determine whether the verb is singular or plural.

**☞ Rule 1:** **"And" always creates a compound subject.**

Q1      An office clerk and a machinist (was / were) present but unhurt by the on-site explosion.

The only connecting word that can make a series of singular nouns into a plural subject is "and." In fact, "and" always creates a plural subject with but one exception, as noted in the next rule.

**☞ Rule 2:** **If two items joined by "and" are deemed to be a single unit, then the subject is considered singular, and a singular verb is required.**

Q2      Eggs and bacon (is / are) Tiffany's favorite breakfast.

**☞ Rule 3:** **When the subject of a sentence consists of two items joined by "or," the subject may either singular or plural. If the two items joined by "or" are both singular, then the subject and verb are singular. If the two items joined by "or" are both plural, then the subject and verb are plural. If one of the two items joined by "or" is singular and the other plural, the verb matches the subject that comes after "or."**

Q3      In the game of chess, capturing one knight or three pawns (yields / yield) the same point value.

**➤ Rule 4:** **"Pseudo-compound subjects" do not make singular subjects plural.**

Pseudo-compound subjects include the following: *as well as, along with, besides, in addition to,* and *together with.*

Q4

A seventeenth-century oil painting, along with several antique vases, (has / have) been placed on the auction block.

**➤ Rule 5:** **Prepositional phrases (i.e., phrases introduced by a preposition) can never contain the subject of a sentence.**

Some of the most common prepositions include *of, in, to, by, for,* and *from.* A definition of the word "preposition," as well as a glossary of other grammatical terms, can be found in the following section titled *Grammatical Munchkins.*

Q5

The purpose of the executive, administrative, and legislative branches of government (is / are) to provide a system of checks and balances.

**➤ Rule 6:** **"There is/there are" and "here is/here are" constructions represent special situations where the verb comes before the subject, not after the subject.**

The normal order in English sentences is subject-verb-object (think S-V-O). "There is/there are" and "here is/here are" sentences are tricky because they create situations in which the verb comes before the subject. Thus, these sentence constructions require that we look past the verb—"is" or "are" in this case—in order to identify the subject.

Q6        Here (is / are) the introduction and chapters one through five.

Q7        (Is / are) there any squash courts available?

*NOTE* ❧ It is a common mistake to use the singular contraction "here's" when referring to a plural subject. Consider this sentence: "Here's the pictures you asked about." The contraction "here's" stands for "here is." The sentence thereby reads: "Here is the pictures you asked about." To correct this, we should avoid the contraction "here's" and write "Here are the pictures you asked about." On the other hand, it would be correct to write: "Here's the list you were looking for." The singular "list" matches the verb "is."

➣ **Rule 7:** **When acting as subjects of a sentence, gerunds and infinitives are always singular and require singular verbs.**

Q8        Entertaining multiple goals (makes / make) a person's life stressful.

➣ **Rule 8:** **"-One," "-body," and "-thing" indefinite pronouns are always singular.**

Q9        One in every three new businesses (fails / fail) within the first five years of operation.

➣ **Rule 9:** **Certain indefinite pronouns—"both," "few," "many," and "several"—are always plural.**

Q10       Few of the students, if any, (is / are) ready for the test.

## CHART OF INDEFINITE PRONOUNS

| Singular or Plural | Examples |
|---|---|
| Certain indefinite pronouns are always singular | anybody, anyone, anything, each, either, every, everybody, everyone, everything, neither, nobody, no one, nothing, one, somebody, someone, something |
| Certain indefinite pronouns are always plural | both, few, many, several |
| Certain indefinite pronouns can be either singular or plural | all, any, most, none, some |

**☞ Rule 10:** **"Some" and "none" indefinite pronouns may be singular or plural.**

Q11     Some of the story (makes / make) sense.

Q12     Some of the comedians (was / were) hilarious.

Q13     None of the candidates (has / have) any previous political experience.

**☞ Rule 11:** **In "either...or" and "neither...nor" constructions, the verb matches the subject which comes directly after the "or" or "nor."**

Q14     Either Johann or Cecilia (is / are) qualified to act as manager.

Q15     Neither management nor workers (is / are) satisfied with the new contract.

**☞ Rule 12:**  **Collective nouns denote a group of individuals (e.g., family, government, assembly, crew). If the collective noun refers to a group as a whole or the idea of oneness predominates, use a singular verb. If not, use a plural verb.**

Q16     Our group (is / are) meeting at 6 p.m.

Q17     A group of latecomers (was / were) escorted to their seats.

**☞ Rule 13:**  **"The number" is a singular noun and takes a singular verb. "A number" is plural and takes a plural verb.**

Q18     The number of road accidents (has / have) decreased.

Q19     A number of train accidents (has / have) occurred.

**☞ Rule 14:**  **Percents or fractions, when followed by an "of phrase," can take a singular or plural verb. The key lies in determining whether the noun within the "of phrase" is singular or plural.**

Q20     Fifty percent of video gaming (is / are) having great reflexes.

Q21     Two-thirds of their classmates (has / have) wakeboards.

☞ Rule 15:    Measurements involving money (e.g., dollars, pounds), time (e.g., five years, the fifties), weight (e.g., pounds, kilograms), or volume (e.g., gallons, kilograms) are always singular and take singular verbs.

Q22    Ten dollars (is / are) an average daily wage for many people in the developing world.

## Pronoun Usage

Problems relating to pronoun usage typically center on personal pronouns. Three areas of confusion may include: choosing between the subjective or objective forms of personal pronouns, making sure pronouns agree in number with their antecedents, and ensuring that pronouns are not ambiguous in context.

☞ Rule 16:    As a general guide, pronouns at or near the front of a sentence take their subjective forms; pronouns at or near the back of a sentence take their objective forms. The precise rule, however, is that pronouns take their subjective form when they are subjects of a verb; they take their objective form when they are objects of a verb.

Q23    The present is from Beth and (she / her).

Q24    Cousin Vinny and (he / him) are both valedictorians.

☞ Rule 17:    Pronouns take their objective form when they are the direct objects of prepositions.

Q25    Between you and (I / me), this plan makes a lot of sense.

Q26    Do not ask for (who / whom) the bell tolls.

Q27    People like you and (I / me) should know better.

## CHART OF PERSONAL PRONOUNS

|  | Subjective | Possessive | Objective |
|---|---|---|---|
| *first-person singular* | I | my, mine | me |
| *second-person singular* | you | your, yours | you |
| *third-person singular* | he, she, it | his, her, hers, its | him, her, it |
| *first-person plural* | we | our, ours | us |
| *second-person plural* | you | your, yours | you |
| *third-person plural* | they | their, theirs | them |
| *who* | who | whose | whom |

**Rule 18:** When forming comparisons using "than" or "as…as," supply any "missing words" (e.g., a verb in the examples below) in order to determine whether the subjective or objective form of the pronoun is correct.

Q28     My nephew is taller than (I / me).

Q29     We skate as fast as (they / them).

Q30     During our group presentation, our teacher asked you more questions than (I / me).

**☞ Rule 19:** **Who vs. Whom. "Who" is the subjective form of the pronoun, and "whom" is the objective form of the pronoun. If "he," "she," or "they" can be substituted for a pronoun in context, the correct form is "who." If "him," "her," or "them" can be substituted for a pronoun in context, the correct form is "whom."**

Q31          The woman (who / whom) is responsible for pension planning is Mrs. Green.

Q32          This gift is intended for (who / whom)?

**☞ Rule 20:** **Do not use a reflexive pronoun (a pronoun ending in "-self") if an ordinary personal pronoun will suffice.**

Q33          The tour leader told Julie and (me / myself) to turn off our cell phones.

Q34          Young Robert hurt (him / himself) while climbing alone.

**☞ Rule 21:** **Pronouns must agree in number with their antecedents.**

Q35          A not-for-profit, like any other organization, has (its / their) own rules and regulations to follow.

Q36          Everybody should mind (his or her / their) own business.

             *NOTE* ᴥ There is something known today as the "singular they." Although it is not considered proper in formal writing (and formal speech), in informal writing (and colloquial speech), it is ever common to see or hear the word "they" used to refer to a singular subject. For example: "Any parent knows that they have to be involved in a child's education." Although "parent" is singular, it is matched with the plural pronoun "they."

**➤ Rule 22:** **Pronouns should not be ambiguous in context. If a pronoun does not refer clearly to a specific noun, it results in a situation of "ambiguous pronoun reference."**

Ambiguous

Sam never argues with his father when <u>he</u> is drunk.

Q37

Sam never argues with his father when _____ is drunk.

**➤ Rule 23:** **"Pronoun shifts," also known as "shifts in point of view," involve the inconsistent matching of pronouns, either in terms of person or number. Within a single sentence (and perhaps within an entire paragraph or writing piece), first person should be matched with first person, second person matched with second person, and third person matched with third person. A common violation involves matching the third-person "one" or "a person" with the second-person "you." Another violation involves matching the third-person singular "he," "she," "one," or "a person" with the third-person plural "they."**

Incorrect

To know that <u>a person</u> can't vote is to know that <u>you don't</u> have a voice.

Q38

To know that a person can't vote is to know that _____ have a voice.

| Incorrect | <u>One</u> cannot really understand another country until <u>they</u> have studied its history and culture. |
| Q39 | One cannot really understand another country until _____ studied its history and culture. |

## Modification

Modifiers, including modifying phrases, must be placed as close as possible to the nouns they modify. As a mostly uninflected language, English depends heavily on word order to establish modifying relationships. Therefore, the position of words is important. Confusion occurs because most modifiers attach themselves to the first thing they can "get their hands on" in the sentence, even if it isn't the right thing.

**☞ Rule 24:** **A misplaced modifier refers to a word which, because of its placement within a sentence, no longer modifies what it originally was intended to modify.**

| Incorrect | He told her he wanted to marry her frequently. |
| Q40 | He _____ told her he wanted to marry her. |
| Incorrect | Coming out of the wood, the janitor was surprised to find termites. |
| Q41 | The janitor was surprised to find termites ____ _____. |

**☞ Rule 25:** **A dangling modifier refers to a situation in which the thing being modified is absent from the sentence.**

| Incorrect | After writing the introduction, the rest of the report was easy. |

Q42                 After writing the introduction, _____ easily drafted the rest of the report.

Incorrect           Walking along the shore, fish could be seen jumping in the lake.

Q43                 Walking along the shore, _____ could see fish jumping in the lake.

**☞ Rule 26:**      **Occasionally, a modifier or modifying phrase may accidentally be placed where it could modify either of the two words or phrases. This situation results in a "squinting modifier." Because it is unclear which of two words or phrases are being modified, the writer should consider rewriting this sentence to clear up this ambiguity.**

Incorrect           She said in her office she had a copy of the map.

Q44                 She said she had _____ lying in her office.

**☞ Rule 27:**      **Whenever a sentence opens with a phrase or clause that is set off by a comma, check to make sure that the first word that follows the comma is properly being modified by the opening phrase or clause that precedes it.**

Incorrect           In addition to building organizational skills, the summer internship also helped me hone my team-building skills.

Q45                 In addition to building organizational skills, _____.

Incorrect           An incredibly complex mechanism, there are some 10 billion nerve cells in the brain.

Q46              An incredibly complex mechanism,
                 _____ has some 10 billion nerve cells.

Incorrect        Based on our observations, the project will
                 succeed.

Q47              _____.

## Parallelism

Parallelism is both a style issue and a grammar issue. In other words, certain elements of parallelism are based on principle and are deemed to be more effective or less effective, better or worse, while other elements are based on rules and are considered correct or incorrect, right or wrong.

The overarching principle regarding parallelism is that similar elements in a sentence must be written in similar form.

☞ **Rule 28:**   **Verbs should follow consistent form. Typically this means that all verbs should end in "-ed" or "-ing."**

Incorrect        In the summer before college, Max <u>was</u> a
                 waiter at a restaurant, <u>pursued</u> magazine sales,
                 and even had a stint at <u>delivering</u> pizzas.

Q48              In the summer before college, Max _____
                 tables, _____ magazines, and even
                 _____ pizzas.

☞ **Rule 29:**   **When prepositions are used before items in a series of three, there are two possibilities with regard to their use. Either a single preposition is used before the first item in a series (but not with the next two items) or prepositions are used before each item in the series.**

| | |
|---|---|
| Incorrect | Our neighbors went <u>to</u> London, Athens, and <u>to</u> Rome. |
| Q49 | Our neighbors went ___ London, Athens, and Rome. |
| Q50 | Our neighbors went ___ London, ___ Athens, and ___ Rome. |

**✒ Rule 30:** **Correlative conjunctions (e.g., "either ... or," "neither ... nor," "not only ... but also," and "both ... and") require that parallelism be maintained after each component part of the correlative.**

| | |
|---|---|
| Incorrect | Jonathan not only likes rugby but also kayaking. |
| Q51 | Jonathan _____ rugby but also kayaking. |
| Q52 | Jonathan _____ rugby but also _____ kayaking. |

**✒ Rule 31:** **Gerunds and infinitives should be presented in parallel form. Where possible, gerunds are matched with gerunds and infinitives are matched with infinitives.**

| | |
|---|---|
| Less effective | <u>Examining</u> the works of William Shakespeare—his plays and poetry—is <u>to marvel</u> at one man's seemingly incomparable depth of literary expression. |
| Q53 | ___ the works of William Shakespeare—his plays and poetry—is <u>to marvel</u> at one man's seemingly incomparable depth of literary expression. |

☞ **Rule 32:** **At times we can acceptably omit words in a sentence and still retain clear meaning. To check for faulty parallelism (in this context it is also known as improper use of ellipsis), complete each sentence component and make sure that each part of the sentence can stand on its own.**

Incorrect | In the *Phantom of the Opera* play, the music is terrific and the stage props superb.

Q54 | In the *Phantom of the Opera* play, the music is terrific and the stage props _____ superb.

Incorrect | The defendant's own testimony on the stand neither contributed nor detracted from his claim of innocence.

Q55 | The defendant's own testimony on the stand neither contributed ___ nor detracted from his claim of innocence.

## Comparisons

The overarching principle in comparisons requires that we compare apples with apples and oranges with oranges.

☞ **Rule 33:** **The superlative ("-est") is used when comparing three or more persons or things; the comparative ("-er") is used when comparing exactly two persons or things.**

Q56 | Between Tom and Brenda, Tom is (better / best) at math.

Q57 | Among our group, Jeff is the (wealthier / wealthiest) person.

Q58                 Of all the roses in our neighborhood,
                    Chauncey Gardiner's grow the (more / most)
                    vigorously.

Q59                 Chauncey Gardiner's roses grow (more
                    / most) vigorously than any other in the
                    neighborhood.

☞ Rule 34:          **Remember to compare the characteristics of
                    one thing to the characteristics of another
                    thing, not the characteristics of one thing
                    directly to another thing.**

Incorrect           Tokyo's population is greater than Beijing.

Q60                 Tokyo's population is greater than the
                    _____ of Beijing.

Q61                 Tokyo's population is greater than Beijing's
                    _____.

Q62                 Tokyo's population is greater than that of
                    _____.

Q63                 Tokyo's population is greater than
                    _____.

Incorrect           Of all the countries contiguous to India,
                    Pakistan's borders are most strongly defended.

Q64                 Of all the countries contiguous to India, _____
                    _____.

☞ Rule 35:          **Faulty or improper comparisons often leave out
                    key words, particularly demonstrative pronouns
                    such as "those" and "that," which are essential
                    to meaning.**

| | |
|---|---|
| Incorrect | The attention span of a dolphin is greater than a chimpanzee. |
| Q65 | The attention span of a dolphin is greater than _____ a chimpanzee. |
| Incorrect | The requirements of a medical degree are more stringent than a law degree. |
| Q66 | The requirements of a medical degree are more stringent than _____ a law degree. |
| Incorrect | Like many politicians, the senator's promises sounded good but ultimately led to nothing. |
| Q67 | Like _____ many politicians, the senator's promises sounded good but ultimately led to nothing. |
| ☞ Rule 36: | **"Like" is used with phrases. "As" is used with clauses. A "phrase" is a group of related words that doesn't have both a subject and a verb. A "clause" is a group of related words that does have a subject and a verb. An easier way to remember the difference is to simply say: "A phrase is a group of words which doesn't have a verb; a clause is a group of words which does have a verb."** |
| Q68 | No one hits home runs (as / like) Barry Bonds. |
| Q69 | No one pitches (as / like) Roy Halladay does. |

## Verb Tenses

### THE SIMPLE AND PROGRESSIVE VERB FORMS

|  | Simple Form | Progressive Form |
|---|---|---|
| *Present Tense* | I travel | I am traveling |
| *Past Tense* | I traveled | I was traveling |
| *Future Tense* | I will travel | I will be traveling |
| *Present Perfect Tense* | I have traveled | I have been traveling |
| *Past Perfect Tense* | I had traveled... | I had been traveling... |
| *Future Perfect Tense* | I will have traveled... | I will have been traveling... |

☞ **Rule 37:** **Consistent use of verb tenses generally requires that a single sentence be written solely in the present, past, or future tense.**

Q70     My dog barks when he (sees / saw) my neighbor's cat.

Q71     Yesterday afternoon, smoke (fills / filled) the sky and sirens sounded.

Q72     Tomorrow, we (will go / will have gone) to the football game.

## VISUALIZING THE SIX VERB TENSES

| Tense | Examples | Summary |
|-------|----------|---------|
| Simple Present | I <u>study</u> physics. | Expresses events or situations that currently exist, including the near past and near present. |
| Simple Past | I <u>studied</u> physics. | Expresses events or situations that existed in the past. |
| Simple Future | I <u>will study</u> physics. | Expresses events or situations that will exist in the future. |
| Present Perfect | I <u>have studied</u> physics. | Expresses events or situations that existed in the past but that touch the present. Look for the verbs "has" or "have." |
| Past Perfect | By the time I graduated from high school, I <u>had decided</u> to study physics. | Expresses events or situations in the past, one of which occurred before the other. Look for the word "had" to signal the first of two past events. |
| Future Perfect | By the time I graduate from college, I <u>will have studied</u> physics for four years. | Expresses events or situations in the future, one of which will occur after the other. Look for the words "will have" to signal the first of two future events. |

**☞ Rule 38:** **The present perfect tense employs the verbs "has" or "have." The past perfect tense employs the auxiliary "had." The future perfect tense employs the verb form "will have."**

Q73     We are raising money for the new scholarship fund. So far we (raised / have raised / had raised) $25,000.

Q74     By the time I began playing golf, I (played / had played) tennis for three hours.

Q75     Larry (studied / has studied / had studied) Russian for five years before he went to work in Moscow.

Q76     By the time evening arrives, we (finished / had finished / will have finished) the task at hand.

**☞ Rule 39:** **The subjunctive mood uses the verb "were" instead of "was." The subjunctive mood is used to indicate a hypothetical situation—it may express a wish, doubt, or possibility. It is also used to indicate a contrary-to-fact situation.**

Q77     Sometimes she wishes she (was / were) on a tropical island having a drink at sunset.

Q78     If I (was / were) you, I would be feeling quite optimistic.

☞ **Rule 40:**  Conditional statements are most commonly expressed in an "If...then" format, in which case an "if" clause is followed by a "results" clause. Confusion often arises as to whether to use "will" or "would." The choice between these verb forms depends on whether a given conditional statement involves the subjunctive. For situations involving the subjunctive, the appropriate verb form is "would." For situations not involving the subjunctive, the verb form is "will." A helpful hint is that "would" is often used in conjunction with "were"—the appearance of both these words within the same sentence is the telltale sign of the subjunctive.

Q79  If economic conditions further deteriorate, public confidence (will / would) plummet.

Q80  If economic conditions were to further deteriorate, public confidence (will / would) plummet.

Q81  If my taxes are less than $10,000, I (will / would) pay that amount immediately.

Q82  If oil (was / were) still abundant, there (will / would) be no energy crisis.

## Diction Review

*Diction may be thought of as "word choices." Choose the answer that conforms to the proper use of diction.*

Q83      (A)      Everyone of the makeup exams is tough, but anyone who misses a scheduled test with good cause is entitled to write one.

             (B)      Every one of the makeup exams is tough, but anyone who misses a scheduled test with good cause is entitled to write one.

             (C)      Every one of the makeup exams is tough, but any one who misses a scheduled test with good cause is entitled to write one.

Q84      (A)      The green book, that is on the top shelf, is the one you need for math. The book which is red is the one you need for writing.

             (B)      The green book, which is on the top shelf, is the one you need for math. The book that is red is the one you need for writing.

             (C)      The green book, which is on the top shelf, is the one you need for math. The book which is red is the one you need for writing.

Q85    (A)    Let's cherish the poem "In Flanders Fields." Remembering those who fought for our freedom lets us live easier.

       (B)    Lets cherish the poem "In Flanders Fields." Remembering those who fought for our freedom let's us live easier.

       (C)    Let's cherish the poem "In Flanders Fields." Remembering those who fought for our freedom let's us live easier.

Q86    (A)    Once we turn these dreaded assignments into the professor's office, we'll feel a lot less obliged to pass any information onto our classmates.

       (B)    Once we turn these dreaded assignments into the professor's office, we'll feel a lot less obliged to pass any information on to our classmates.

       (C)    Once we turn these dreaded assignments in to the professor's office, we'll feel a lot less obliged to pass any information on to our classmates.

Q87    (A)    The McCorkendales didn't used to enjoy warm weather, but that was before they moved to Morocco and got used to summer temperatures as high as 35 degrees Celsius.

(B)   The McCorkendales didn't <u>use to</u>
      enjoy warm weather, but that was
      before they moved to Morocco and got
      <u>use to</u> summer temperatures as high
      as 35 degrees Celsius.

(C)   The McCorkendales didn't <u>use to</u>
      enjoy warm weather, but that was
      before they moved to Morocco and got
      <u>used to</u> summer temperatures as high
      as 35 degrees Celsius.

## Idioms Review

*Idioms may be thought of as "word expressions." Idioms, like grammar
and diction, are correct or incorrect, right or wrong. Here are fifteen
common idioms. Choose the answer that is idiomatically correct.*

Q88   (A)   A choice must be made <u>between</u> blue
            <u>and</u> green.

      (B)   A choice must be made <u>between</u> blue
            <u>or</u> green.

Q89   (A)   Many doctors <u>consider</u> stress a more
            destructive influence on one's longev
            ity than smoking, drinking, or over
            eating.

      (B)   Many doctors <u>consider</u> stress <u>as</u> a
            more destructive influence on one's
            longevity than smoking, drinking, or
            overeating.

(C)    Many doctors <u>consider</u> stress <u>to be</u> a more destructive influence on one's longevity than smoking, drinking, or overeating.

Q90    (A)    At first women were <u>considered</u> at low risk for HIV.

(B)    At first women were <u>considered as</u> at low risk for HIV.

(C)    At first women were <u>considered to be</u> at low risk for HIV.

Q91    (A)    Many <u>credit</u> Gutenberg <u>as having</u> invented the printing press.

(B)    Many <u>credit</u> Gutenberg <u>with having</u> invented the printing press.

Q92    (A)    In the movie *Silence of the Lambs*, Dr. Hannibal Lecter is <u>depicted as</u> a brilliant psychiatrist and cannibalistic serial killer who is confined as much by the steel bars of his cell as by the prison of his own mind.

(B)    In the movie *Silence of the Lambs*, Dr. Hannibal Lecter is <u>depicted to be</u> a brilliant psychiatrist and cannibalistic serial killer who is confined as much by the steel bars of his cell as by the prison of his own mind.

93     (A)     Only experts can <u>distinguish</u> a master-piece <u>and</u> a fake.

        (B)     Only experts can <u>distinguish</u> a master-piece <u>from</u> a fake.

Q94     (A)     Although medical practitioners have the technology to perform brain transplants, there is no clear evidence that they can <u>do it</u>.

        (B)     Although medical practitioners have the technology to perform brain transplants, there is no clear evidence that they can <u>do so</u>.

Q95     (A)     <u>In comparison to</u> France, Luxembourg is an amazingly small country.

        (B)     <u>In comparison with</u> France, Luxembourg is an amazingly small country.

Q96     (A)     Roger Federer won Wimbledon with a classic tennis style, <u>in contrast to</u> Bjorn Borg, who captured his titles using an unorthodox playing style.

        (B)     Roger Federer won Wimbledon with a classic tennis style, <u>in contrast with</u> Bjorn Borg, who captured his titles using an unorthodox playing style.

Q97     (A)     There is <u>more</u> talk of a single North American currency today <u>compared to</u> ten years ago.

(B)    There is <u>more</u> talk of a single North American currency today <u>compared with</u> ten years ago.

(C)    There is <u>more</u> talk of a single North American currency today <u>than</u> ten years ago.

Q98

(A)    I <u>prefer</u> blackjack <u>over</u> poker.

(B)    I <u>prefer</u> blackjack <u>to</u> poker.

Q99

(A)    Rembrandt is <u>regarded as</u> the greatest painter of the Renaissance period.

(B)    Rembrandt is <u>regarded to be</u> the greatest painter of the Renaissance period.

Q100

(A)    The speaker does a good job of <u>tying</u> motivational theory <u>to</u> obtainable results.

(B)    The speaker does a good job of <u>tying</u> motivational theory <u>with</u> obtainable results.

## Answers to the 100-Question Quiz

Q1      An office clerk and a machinist <u>were</u> present but unhurt by the on-site explosion.

Q2      Eggs and bacon <u>is</u> Tiffany's favorite breakfast.

The words "eggs" and "bacon" are intimately connected and deemed to be a signal unit.

Q3      In the game of chess, capturing one knight or three pawns <u>yield</u> the same point value

The subject "pawns" is plural and requires the plural verb "are."

Q4      A seventeenth-century oil painting, along with several antique vases, <u>has</u> been placed on the auction block.

Q5      The purpose of the executive, administrative, and legislative branches of government <u>is</u> to provide a system of checks and balances.

The subject of the sentence is "purpose." The prepositional phrase "of the executive, administrative, and legislative branches of government" does not affect the verb choice.

Q6      Here <u>are</u> the introduction and chapters one through five.

The compound subject "introduction *and* chapters one through five" necessitates using the plural verb "are."

Q7      <u>Are</u> there any squash courts available?

One helpful tip is to first express this as a declarative sentence: "There are squash courts available." Now it is easier to see that the subject is plural—squash courts—and a plural verb *are* is appropriate.

Q8    Entertaining multiple goals <u>makes</u> a person's life stressful.

"Entertaining multiple goals" is a gerund phrase that acts as the subject of the sentence (singular).

Q9    One in every three new businesses <u>fails</u> within the first five years of operation.

Q10   Few of the students, if any, <u>are</u> ready for the test.

The phrase "if any" is parenthetical, and in no way affects the plurality of the sentence.

Q11   Some of the story <u>makes</u> sense.

Q12   Some of the comedians <u>were</u> hilarious.

Q13   None of the candidates <u>have</u> any previous political experience.

Note that if "neither" was used in place of "none," the correct sentence would read: "Neither of the candidates <u>has</u> any political experience." "Neither" is an indefinite pronoun that is always singular. "None" is an indefinite pronoun that is singular or plural depending on context. The fact that "none" takes "have" and "neither" would take "has" is indeed a peculiarity.

Q14   Either Johann or Cecilia <u>is</u> qualified to act as manager.

Q15    Neither management nor workers <u>are</u> satisfied with the new contract.

Q16    Our group <u>is</u> meeting at 6 p.m.

Q17    A group of latecomers <u>were</u> escorted to their seats.

Q18    The number of road accidents <u>has</u> decreased.

Q19    A number of train accidents <u>have</u> occurred.

Q20    Fifty percent of video gaming <u>is</u> having great reflexes.

Q21    Two-thirds of their classmates <u>have</u> wakeboards.

Q22    Ten dollars <u>is</u> an average daily wage for many people in the developing word.

Q23    The present is from Beth and <u>her</u>.

Q24    Cousin Vinny and <u>he</u> are both valedictorians.

Q25    Between you and <u>me</u>, this plan makes a lot of sense.

       The pronoun "me" (the objective form of the pronoun "I") is the direct object of the preposition "between."

Q26    Do not ask for <u>whom</u> the bell tolls.

       The pronoun "whom" (the objective form of the pronoun "who") is the direct object of the preposition "for."

Q27    People like you and <u>me</u> should know better.

The objective form of the pronoun—"me"—must follow the preposition "like."

Q28    My nephew is taller than I.

In order to test this: My nephew is taller than I am.

Q29    We skate as fast as they.

Test this: We skate as fast as they do.

Q30    During our group presentation, our teacher asked you more questions than me.

Test this: During our group presentation, our teacher asked you more questions than she or he asked me.

Q31    The woman who is responsible for pension planning is Mrs. Green.

*She* is responsible for city planning; "he/she" is substitutable for "who."

Q32    This gift is intended for whom?

The gift is intended for *him* or *her*; "him/her" is substitutable for "whom."

Q33    The tour leader told Julie and me to turn off our cell phones.

Q34    Young Robert hurt himself while climbing alone.

Q35    A not-for-profit, like any other organization, has its own rules and regulations to follow.

Q36    Everybody should mind his or her own business.

Q37    Sam never argues with his father when <u>Sam</u> is drunk.

The sentence "Sam never argues with his father when he is drunk" is grammatically correct but contextually vague. It is contextually vague because we feel that it is Sam who is drunk whereas, grammatically, it is Sam's father who is actually drunk (a pronoun modifies the nearest noun that came before it; here the pronoun "he" modifies the noun "father"). The sentence needs to be rephrased to clear up potential ambiguity. The most direct way to achieve this is to replace the pronoun "he" with the noun it is intended to refer to, namely Sam. Note that another way to clear up this ambiguity is to restructure this sentence as follows: "When <u>he</u> is drunk, Sam never argues with his father."

Q38    To know that a person can't vote is to know that <u>he or she doesn't</u> have a voice.

A "person" is a noun in the third person and the correct answer must be a pronoun that matches it in the third person.

Other correct options would include:

To know that a person can't vote is to know that <u>a person doesn't</u> have a voice.

To know that a person can't vote is to know that <u>one doesn't</u> have a voice.

Q39    One cannot really understand another country until <u>one has</u> studied its history and culture.

We have essentially five ways to validate this sentence—"one has," "a person has," "he has," "she has," or "he or she has." In the latter option, using "he or she has" keeps writing gender neutral (politically correct). The grammatical reason that the original does the work is because "one" is a third-person singular pronoun while "they" is a third-person plural pronoun. Thus, we have a pronoun shift or a shift in viewpoint. Any answer must also be in the third-person singular. Given the opportunity to rewrite the original sentence, two other correct options would also include:

You cannot really understand another country unless <u>you have</u> studied its history and culture.

Here, the second-person pronoun "you" is matched with the second-person pronoun "you."

We cannot really understand another country unless <u>we have</u> studied its history and culture. Here the first-person plural pronoun "we" is matched with the first-person plural pronoun "we."

Q40    He <u>frequently</u> told her he wanted to marry her.

Q41    The janitor was surprised to find termites <u>coming out of the wood</u>.

Q42    After writing the introduction, <u>I</u> easily drafted the rest of the report.

Q43    Walking along the shore, <u>the couple</u> could see fish jumping in the lake.

Q44    She said she had <u>a copy of the map</u> lying in her office.

She is presently not in her office but the map is.

Also: While we were sitting in her office, she told me she had a copy of the map.

She is in her office with or without the map.

Q45      In addition to building organizational skills, <u>I also honed my team-building skills during the summer internship</u>.

Q46      An incredibly complex mechanism, <u>the brain</u> has some 10 billion nerve cells.

Q47      <u>On the basis of our observations, we believe the project will succeed</u>.

Firstly, "the project" is not based on our observations. Observations must be made by people, so "we" is an appropriate substitute. Secondly, the phrase "based on" is incorrect because we cannot be physically standing on our observations or attached to them. The correct phraseology is "on the basis of." In general, "based on" is not an appropriate modifier to use with people; but it's fine for inanimate objects, e.g., a movie based on a book.

Q48      In the summer before college, Max <u>waited</u> tables, <u>sold</u> magazines, and even <u>delivered</u> pizzas.

Q49      Our neighbors went <u>to</u> London, Athens, and Rome.

Q50      Our neighbors went <u>to</u> London, <u>to</u> Athens, and <u>to</u> Rome.

Q51      Jonathan likes <u>not only</u> rugby <u>but also</u> kayaking.

Here the verb "likes" is placed before the "not only...but also" correlative conjunction, creating parallelism between the words "rugby" and "kayaking."

Q52    Jonathan <u>not only likes</u> rugby <u>but also likes</u> kayaking.

Here, the verb "likes" is repeated after each component part of the "not only ... but also" construction. Thus the words "likes rugby" and "likes kayaking" are parallel.

Q53    <u>To examine</u> the works of William Shakespeare—his plays and poetry—is <u>to marvel</u> at one man's seemingly incomparable depth of literary expression.

The infinitives "to examine" and "to marvel" are parallel.

Q54    In the *Phantom of the Opera* play, the music <u>is</u> terrific and the stage props <u>are</u> superb.

Since the verbs are different (i.e., "is" and "are"), we must write them out.

*NOTE* ✍ Rules of ellipsis govern the acceptable omission of words in writing and speech. There is no need to say, "Paris <u>is</u> a large and <u>is</u> an exciting city." We can say, "Paris <u>is</u> a large and an exciting city." The verb (i.e., "is") is the same throughout the sentence, so there's no need to write it out a second time. Note, however, that the articles "a" and "an" are different and must be written out. Omitting the "an" in the second half of the sentence would result in an incorrect sentence: "Paris is a large and exciting city."

Q55        The defendant's own testimony on the stand neither contributed <u>to</u> nor detracted from his claim of innocence.

Since the prepositions are different, we cannot omit either of them

*NOTE* ❧ As a follow-up example, there is no need to say, "*The Elements of Style* <u>was written by</u> William Strunk, Jr., and <u>was written by</u> E. B. White." Since the verb form "was written" and the preposition "by" are the same when applied to both authors, we can simply say, "*The Elements of Style* was written by William Strunk, Jr., and E. B. White."

Q56        Between Tom and Brenda, Tom is <u>better</u> at math.

Q57        Among our group, Jeff is the <u>wealthiest</u> person.

Q58        Of all the roses grown in our neighborhood, Chauncey Gardiner's grow the <u>most</u> vigorously.

Q59        Chauncey Gardiner's roses grow <u>more</u> vigorously than any other in the neighborhood.

Q60        Tokyo's population is greater than the <u>population</u> of Beijing.

Q61        Tokyo's population is greater than Beijing's <u>population</u>.

Q62        Tokyo's population is greater than that of <u>Beijing</u>.

In the above example, the demonstrative pronoun "that" substitutes for the words "the population," and we are effectively saying: "Tokyo's population is greater than <u>the population</u> of Beijing."

*NOTE* ❦ It is incorrect to write: "Tokyo's population is greater than that of Beijing's." Such a sentence would read: "Tokyo's population is greater than the population of Beijing's (population)."

Q63 Tokyo's population is greater than Beijing's.

Also: Tokyo's population is greater than Beijing's population.

Also: Tokyo's population is greater than that of Beijing.

Also: Tokyo's population is greater than the population of Beijing.

Q64 Of all the countries contiguous to India, Pakistan has the most strongly defended borders.

The following would not be a correct solution: "Of all the countries contiguous to India, the borders of Pakistan are most strongly defended."

Q65 The attention span of a dolphin is greater than that of a chimpanzee.

Q66 The requirements of a medical degree are more stringent than those of a law degree.

Q67 Like those of many politicians, the senator's promises sounded good but ultimately led to nothing.

Alternatively, we could use the words "like the promises of" in the following manner: "Like the promises of many politicians, the senator's promises sounded good but ultimately led to nothing." Ignoring the fill-in-the-blank, we could also write: "Like many politicians' promises, the senator's promises..."

Q68     No one hits home runs <u>like</u> Barry Bonds.

"Like Barry Bonds" is a phrase. A phrase is a group of words that lacks a verb.

Q69     No one pitches <u>as</u> Roy Halladay does.

"As Roy Halladay does" is a clause. A clause is a group of words that contains a verb.

Q70     My dog barks when he <u>sees</u> my neighbor's cat.

The simple present tense "barks" is consistent with the simple present tense "sees."

Q71     Yesterday afternoon, smoke <u>filled</u> the sky and sirens sounded.

The simple past tense verb "filled" is consistent with the simple past tense verb "sounded."

Q72     Tomorrow, we <u>will go</u> to the football game.

Q73     We are raising money for the new scholarship fund. So far we <u>have raised</u> $25,000.

Q74     By the time I began playing golf, I <u>had played</u> tennis for three hours.

The playing of tennis precedes the playing of golf for these two past tense events.

Q75     Larry <u>had studied</u> Russian for five years before he went to work in Moscow.

The past perfect tense is constructed using the auxiliary "had" and the past participle of the verb, in this case "studied." The past perfect tense clarifies the sequence of two past tense events. Here, it is clear that Larry first studied Russian and then went to Moscow.

Question: What is the difference between the following two sentences?

1) Larry <u>had studied</u> Russian for five years before he went to work in Moscow.

2) Larry <u>studied</u> Russian for five years before he went to work in Moscow.

Most grammar experts side with sentence 1 as the correct and preferable choice. However, some experts would argue that sentence 2 is equally correct. Sentence 2 uses two past tense verbs (i.e., "studied" and "went") as well as the temporal word "before." It can be argued that the combined use of the past perfect "had" and temporal words (e.g., *before, after, previously, prior, subsequently*), as seen in sentence 1, creates a redundancy, and that when the sequence of two past tense events is clear, particularly through the use of temporal word(s), the use of the past perfect tense is considered optional.

*NOTE* ✧ To clear up some of the confusion surrounding use of the word "had," let's review its main uses. First, "had" is used as an actual verb and functions as the past tense of the verb "to have." Examples: "I have 500 dollars" versus "I had 500 dollars." In the previous example, "had" is a verb meaning "to possess." It also functions as a verb meaning "to experience" or "to undergo." Examples: "I had a good time at the party" or "I had a bad headache." It also functions as a verb meaning "to be required to." Example: "I had to go to the store today to get some medicine for my mother."

As already mentioned, one important use of the auxiliary "had" is to form the past perfect tense. Additionally, the auxiliary "had" can also play a role in forming the subjunctive ("I wish I had done things differently") and the conditional ("If I had known then what I know now, things might have been different.")

Confusion may arise in situations involving the use of "had had." The past perfect is formed by using the auxiliary "had" plus the past participle of a verb. In situations involving the verb "had," the past perfect tense becomes "had had." Example: "By the time he turned twenty-five, he had had six different jobs." Here, the act of working at six different jobs occurs prior to turning twenty-five years of age, and the past perfect tense is invoked to clarify the sequence of events. One way to avoid employing two "had's" is to change the verb, when applicable. In this case, we could write, "By the time he turned twenty-five, he had worked at six different jobs."

One common mistake is to place "had" before past tense verbs. The reality is that many everyday writers now associate "had" with the past tense, and thus "sprinkle" it in front of many past tense verbs. Consider the following two statements:

1) "He <u>worked</u> in the diplomatic corps."
2) "He <u>had worked</u> in the diplomatic corps."

Only the first statement is grammatically correct. The second statement (standing alone), although colloquial, is not grammatically sound. Statement 1 is the simple past tense. He worked in the diplomatic corps for a specific period of time in the past, but doesn't anymore. Statement 2, to the casual ear, carries a meaning nearly identical to statement 1. It appears that many everyday writers prefer statement 2 to statement 1, a likely reason being that it may sound better to one's ears.

A good rule of thumb is to omit the use of "had" if it isn't needed. Instead of writing "I <u>had</u> thought a lot about what you said," write "I thought a lot about what you said." A past tense verb does not need the help of the auxiliary "had" to do its job. That said, since so many writers now associate "had" with the simple past tense, the practice of placing "had's" in front of past tense verbs is likely so entrenched that the practice is here to stay.

This phenomenon might be referred to as "invoking" the past perfect tense. It describes situations in which the past perfect tense is substituted for the simple past tense. Consider the following pairings:

1) They <u>went</u> to Santa Catalina Island many times.
2) They <u>had gone</u> to Santa Catalina Island many times.

1) She <u>grew</u> her hair long.
2) She <u>had grown</u> her hair long.

1) He <u>was</u> a civil servant.
2) He <u>had been</u> a civil servant.

All three of the previous word pairings sound very much equivalent. It is essentially a draw between the simple past tense ("went" or "grew" or "was") and the auxiliary "had" + past participle ("had gone" or "had grown" or "had been"). The point here is that it is understandable why writers might choose to invoke the past perfect tense even though there are no grammatical grounds for doing so. As a practical matter, writers should feel free to use whatever form sounds better. To be clear, each of these "second" sentences could represent legitimate examples of the past perfect tense given additional context. Cases in point: "Before moving to Oregon, they had gone to Santa Catalina Island many times" ... "By the time she entered high school, she had grown her hair long" ... "He had been a civil servant until deciding to start his own business."

A close cousin of the "invoked" past perfect may be called the "invoked" present perfect. It describes situations in which the present perfect tense is substituted for the simple past tense. Consider the following trio:

1) I <u>have misplaced</u> my car keys.
2) I <u>misplaced</u> my car keys.
3) I <u>had misplaced</u> my car keys.

Statement 2 is the simple past tense and it could be argued, on grounds of logic, that it represents the only grammatically sound statement. Statement 3 is an example of the "invoked" past perfect tense, which involves using the past perfect tense when the past tense is needed; it is in common use but, as mentioned, is arguably not technically correct. Statement 1 is an example of the "invoked" present perfect tense. The question becomes: What does statement 1 really mean? In reality, either I misplaced my car keys or I didn't misplace my car keys. If I really did misplace my car keys, then why isn't statement 1, written in the simple past tense, sufficient to express this idea?

Many writers likely "invoke" the present perfect
tense, as seen in statement 1 above, because it
sounds right. This may be an apt illustration
of how the written English language is being
influenced by the way we speak it and hear it being
spoken. The use of "have misplaced" (present
perfect tense) likely makes the event seem as
if it occurred only a short time ago. The use of
"misplaced" (past tense) makes the event seem as
if occurred at a time further in the past. The use of
"had misplaced" (past perfect tense) makes it seem
as if the event occurred at a time in the yet more
distant past.

In summary, the use of both the "invoked" past
perfect and the "invoked" present perfect is
very much entrenched in everyday writing and
speech. With respect to the above-mentioned
three statements, readers are likely to see similar
examples used interchangeably.

Q76     By the time evening arrives, we <u>will have finished</u>
the task at hand.

The future act of finishing the task at hand will
occur before evening arrives.

Q77     Sometimes she wishes she <u>were</u> on a tropical
island having a drink at sunset.

Expresses a wish; the subjunctive "were," not
"was," is the correct choice.

Q78     If I <u>were</u> you, I would be feeling quite optimistic.

Indicates a hypothetical, contrary-to-fact situation;
"were," not "was," is the correct choice.

Q79    If economic conditions further deteriorate, public confidence <u>will</u> plummet.

"Will" is correct in future events with implied certainty; we are making a statement about the future in absolute terms. The sentence is written in the form of "If $x$ happens, then $y$ will happen."

Q80    If economic conditions were to further deteriorate, public confidence <u>would</u> plummet.

Note that the inclusion of "were," when coupled with "would," signals the subjunctive mood.

Q81    If my taxes are less than $10,000, I <u>will</u> pay that amount immediately.

"Will" is correct when dealing with future events with implied certainty.

Q82    If oil <u>were</u> still abundant, there <u>would</u> be no energy crisis.

This situation is clearly contrary to fact. Oil is not abundant, and there is an energy crisis; "were" and "would" are used to signal the subjunctive.

Q83    Choice B
<u>Every one</u> of the makeup exams is tough, but <u>anyone</u> who misses a scheduled test with good cause is entitled to write one.

The words *anyone* and *any one* are not interchangeable. *Anyone* means "any person" whereas *any one* means "any single person or thing." Likewise, the words *everyone* and *every one* are not interchangeable. *Everyone* means "everybody in a group" whereas *every one* means "each person."

Q84    Choice B
The green book, <u>which</u> is on the top shelf, is the
one you need for math. The book <u>that</u> is red is the
one you need for grammar.

It is common practice to use *which* with nonrestrictive (nonessential) phrases or clauses and
to use *that* with restrictive (essential) phrases
or clauses. Nonrestrictive phrases are typically
enclosed with commas, whereas restrictive phrases
are never enclosed with commas. "Which is on the
top shelf" is a nonrestrictive (nonessential) phrase.
It is optional. We can omit it, and the sentence
will still make sense. "That is red" is a restrictive
(essential) phrase. It is not optional. Without it the
sentence will not make sense.

Q85    Choice A
<u>Let's</u> cherish the poem "In Flanders Fields."
Remembering those who fought for our freedom
<u>lets</u> us live easier.

*Let's* is a contraction for "let us"; *lets* is a verb
meaning "to allow" or "to permit." This sentence
could have been rewritten: <u>Let us</u> cherish the
poem "In Flanders Fields." Remembering those
who fought for our freedom *allows* us to live easier.

Q86    Choice C
Once we turn these dreaded assignments <u>in to</u> the
professor's office, we'll feel a lot less obliged to
pass information <u>on to</u> our classmates.

The words *into* and *in to* are not interchangeable.
Likewise, the words *onto* and *on to* are not interchangeable. Case in point: Turning assignments
*into* the professor's office is a magician's trick!
Passing information *onto* our classmates would
mean physically putting the information on them.

Q87        Choice C
The McCorkendales didn't <u>use to</u> fancy warm weather, but that was before they moved to Morocco and got <u>used to</u> summer temperatures as high as 35 degrees Celsius.

Although *used to* and *use to* are largely interchangeable in spoken English, because the letter "d" is inaudible in many oral contexts, this is not the case in formal writing. The correct form for habitual action is *used to*, not *use to*. Example: "We <u>used to</u> go to the movies all the time." However, when *did* precedes "use(d) to" the correct form is "use to." This is commonly the case in questions and negative constructions. Example: Didn't you <u>use to</u> live on a farm? I didn't <u>use to</u> daydream.

Q88        Choice A
Idiom: *Between X and Y*

A choice must be made <u>between</u> blue <u>and</u> green.

Q89        Choice A
Idiom: *Consider(ed)* – not followed by *"to be"*

Many doctors <u>consider</u> stress a more destructive influence on one's longevity than smoking, drinking, or overeating.

*Consider/considered* is not followed by "to be" (or "as") when *consider(ed)* is followed by a direct object and used in the sense that some person or organization considers something to have some perceived quality. The word "stress" functions as a direct object of the verb *consider*, and the perceived quality is the "destructive influence" of stress.

Q90       Choice C
Idiom: *Consider(ed)* – followed by *"to be"*

At first women were <u>considered to be</u> at low risk for HIV.

*Consider/considered* is followed by "to be" when *consider(ed)* has the meaning of "believed to be" or "thought to be."

Q91       Choice B
Idioms: *Credit(ed) X with having*

Many <u>credit</u> Gutenberg <u>with having</u> invented the printing press.

Q92       Choice A
Idiom: *Depicted as*

In the movie *Silence of the Lambs,* Dr. Hannibal Lecter is <u>depicted as</u> a brilliant psychiatrist and cannibalistic serial killer who is confined as much by the steel bars of his cell as by the prison of his own mind.

Q93       Choice B
Idiom: *Distinguish X from Y*

Only experts can <u>distinguish</u> a masterpiece <u>from</u> a fake.

Q94       Choice B
Idiom: *Do so*

Although doctors have the technology to perform brain transplants, there is no clear evidence that they can <u>do so</u>.

Q95         Choice A
            Idiom: *In comparison to*

            <u>In comparison to</u> France, Luxembourg is an
            amazingly small country.

Q96         Choice A
            Idiom: *In contrast to*

            Roger Federer won Wimbledon with a classic
            tennis style, <u>in contrast to</u> Bjorn Borg, who
            captured his titles using an unorthodox playing
            style.

Q97         Choice C
            Idiom: *More...than/(Less...than)*

            There is <u>more</u> talk of a single North American
            currency today <u>than</u> ten years ago.

Q98         Choice B
            Idiom: *Prefer X to Y*

            I <u>prefer</u> blackjack <u>to</u> poker.

Q99         Choice A
            Idiom: *Regarded as*

            Rembrandt is <u>regarded as</u> the greatest painter of
            the Renaissance period.

Q100        Choice A
            Idiom: *Tying X to Y*

            The speaker does a good job of <u>tying</u> motivational
            theory <u>to</u> obtainable results.

# Grammatical Munchkins

This section contains a repository of grammatical terms that serves as a glossary, replete with clarifying examples. The value of this section lies in its ability to provide a convenient summary of important terms as well as a jumping-off point—a means of engendering interest—for those readers wishing to pursue more in-depth study.

## The Eight Parts of Speech

There are eight parts of speech in English: nouns, pronouns, verbs, adjectives, adverbs, prepositions, conjunctions, and interjections.

**Noun**

A noun is a word that names a person, place, thing, or idea.

Example: <u>Sally</u> is a nice person and you can speak freely with her.

**Pronoun**

A pronoun is a word used in place of a noun or another pronoun.

Example: Sally is a nice person and <u>you</u> can speak freely with <u>her</u>.

**Verb**

A verb is a word that expresses an action or a state of being.

Example: Sally <u>is</u> a nice person and you <u>can speak</u> freely with her.

**Adjective**

An adjective is a word used to modify or describe a noun or pronoun.

Example: Sally is a <u>nice</u> person and you can speak freely with her. The adjective "nice" modifies the noun "person."

**Adverb**

An adverb is a word that modifies an adjective, a verb, or another adverb.

Example: Sally is a nice person and you can speak <u>freely</u> with her. The word "freely" modifies the verb "speak."

**Preposition**

A preposition is a word that shows a relationship between two or more words.

Example: Sally is a nice person and you can speak freely <u>with</u> her.

Prepositions are sometimes informally referred to as words that describe "the directions a squirrel can go." Squirrels, after all, seem to be able to run, climb, or crawl in nearly every possible direction.

Examples of prepositions include: *after, against, at, before, between, by, concerning, despite, down, for, from, in, of, off, on, onto, out, over, through, to, under, until, up, with.*

**Conjunction**

A conjunction is a word that joins or connects words, phrases, clauses, or sentences. Three major types of conjunctions include coordinating conjunctions, subordinating conjunctions, and correlative conjunctions.

Example: Sally is a nice person <u>and</u> you can speak freely with her.

| | |
|---|---|
| **Interjection** | An interjection is a word or a term that denotes a strong or sudden feeling. Interjections are usually, but not always, followed by an exclamation mark. |
| | Example: Sally is a nice person and you can speak freely with her. <u>Wow!</u> |

## Parts of Speech vs. The Seven Characteristics

Each of the eight parts of speech has one or more of the following characteristics: (1) gender, (2) number, (3) person, (4) case, (5) voice, (6) mood, and (7) tense. The matching of a particular part of speech with its relevant characteristics is the primary "cause" of grammar.

*NOTE* ⋗ Adjectives, adverbs, prepositions, conjunctions, and interjections do not have gender, number, person, case, voice, mood, or tense. Only nouns, pronouns, and verbs have one or more of these seven characteristics.

| | |
|---|---|
| **Gender** | Gender may be feminine or masculine. Only nouns and pronouns have gender. |
| | Examples: Masculine—"boy" (noun), "him" (pronoun). Feminine—"girl" (noun), "her" (pronoun). |
| **Number** | Number may be singular or plural. Only nouns, pronouns, and verbs have number. |
| | Examples: Singular—"home" (noun), "I" (pronoun), "plays" (verb). Plural—"homes" (noun), "we" (pronoun), "play" (verb). |

**Person**

Person may be first person, second person, or third person. A person doing the speaking is considered first person; the person spoken to is considered second person; a person spoken about is considered third person. Only pronouns and verbs have person.

Examples: First person—"I write" (pronoun + verb). Second person—"you write" (pronoun + verb). Third person—"he writes" (pronoun + verb).

*NOTE* ∾ When verbs are matched with personal pronouns, verbs differ only in number with respect to third-person singular pronouns. In the third-person singular, verbs are formed with the letter "s." For example: "He or she travels." But: "I travel," "you travel," and "they travel."

**Case**

Case may be subjective, objective, or possessive. Only nouns and pronouns have case.

Examples: Subjective—"Felix has a cat." ("Felix" is a noun); "He has a cat." ("he" is a pronoun). Objective—"The cat scratched Felix." ("Felix" is a noun); "The cat scratched him." ("him" is a pronoun). Possessive—"Felix's cat has amber eyes." (Felix's is a noun); "His cat has amber eyes." ("his" is a pronoun).

*NOTE* ∾ Although nouns have case, noun forms remain virtually unchanged in the subjective, objective, and possessive cases.

**Voice**

Voice may be active or passive. Only verbs have voice.

Examples: Active voice—"You mailed a letter." Passive voice—"The letter was mailed by you."

*NOTE* ✍ In the active voice, the doer of the action is placed at the front of the sentence; the receiver of the action is placed at the back of the sentence. In the passive voice, the receiver of the action is placed at the front of the sentence while the doer of the action is relegated to the back of the sentence.

**Mood**

Mood can be described as being indicative, imperative, or subjunctive. Only verbs have mood.

Examples: Indicative mood (makes a statement or asks a question)—"It's a nice day." Imperative mood (makes a request or gives a command)—"Please sit down." Subjunctive mood (expresses a wish or a contrary-to-fact situation)—"I wish I were in Hawaii."

**Tense**

Tense refers to time. There are six tenses in English—present tense, past tense, future tense, present perfect tense, past perfect tense, and future perfect tense. Each of these six tenses occurs within two forms: the simple form and the progressive form.

Examples: Present tense in the simple form—"I study." Present tense in the progressive form—"I am studying."

## Other Grammatical Terms

**Adjective clause**  An adjective clause is a subordinate clause that, like an adjective, modifies a noun or pronoun.

Example: "The house that sits on top of the hill is painted in gold." The adjective clause "that sits on top of the hill" describes the "house."

**Antecedent**  An antecedent is the word to which a pronoun refers. It is the word that the pronoun is effectively taking the place of.

Example: "The clock is broken; it is now being repaired." The pronoun "it" is substituting for the antecedent "clock."

**Appositive phrase**  An appositive phrase is used merely for description and is typically set off by commas.

Example: "The world's oldest book, which was discovered in a tomb, is 2,500 years old."

**Article**  An article serves to identify certain nouns. English has three articles: *a, an, the. The* is known as a definite article; *a* and *an* are known as indefinite articles. Articles are often erroneously referred to as one of the eight parts of speech.

**Clause**  A clause is a group of related words that does have a subject and a verb.

Example: "Many people believe in psychics even though they never hear of a psychic winning the lottery." The previous sentence contains two clauses. The first clause—"many people believe in psychics"—is an independent clause, containing the subject "people" and the verb "believe." The second clause—"even though they never hear of a psychic winning the lottery"—is a dependent clause, containing the subject "they" and the verb "winning."

**Collective noun**

Collective nouns are nouns which represent a group.

Examples: *audience, band, bunch, class, committee, couple, crowd, family, group, herd, jury, majority, people, percent, personnel, team.*

**Complement**

A complement is something that completes a subject and verb. Not all sentences have complements.

Examples: "I am."—This three-letter sentence (incidentally the shortest in the English language) does not contain a complement. "I am fit."—This sentence does contain a complement; the complement is the word "fit."

**Coordinating conjunction**

Coordinating conjunctions join clauses of equal weight.

Examples: There are seven coordinating conjunctions in English—*and, but, yet, or, nor, for,* and *so.*

**Correlative conjunction**

Correlative conjunctions join clauses or phrases of equal weight. They also impose a sense of logic.

Examples: *either ... or, neither ... nor, not only ... but (also)*, and *both ... and*. The word "also" appears in brackets because it is deemed optional.

**Demonstrative pronoun**

Demonstrative pronouns serve to point out persons or things.

Example: There are four demonstrative pronouns in English: *this, that, these*, and *those*.

**Dependent clause**

A dependent clause is a clause that cannot stand on its own as a complete sentence. Dependent clauses are sometimes called subordinate clauses.

Example: "Keep an umbrella with you because it's forecast for rain." The dependent clause is "because it's forecast for rain."

**Direct object**

A direct object (of a verb) receives the action of that verb or shows the result of that action.

Example: "The outfielder caught the ball." The word "ball" is the direct object of the verb "caught."

See also Indirect Object.

**Gerund**

Gerunds are verb forms that end in "ing" and function as nouns. Informally they may be referred to as "words that look like verbs but function as nouns."

Examples: "Eating vegetables is good for you." "Learning languages is rewarding." "Seeing is believing." Note that "eating," "learning," "seeing," and "believing" are all gerunds.

**Indefinite pronoun**

Indefinite pronouns are pronouns that do not refer to a specific antecedent.

A more complete list of indefinite pronouns includes: *all, any, anybody, anyone, anything, both, each, either, every, everybody, everyone, everything, few, many, most, neither, nobody, none, no one, nothing, one, several, some, somebody, someone,* and *something.*

**Independent clause**

An independent clause is a clause that can stand on its own as a complete sentence. Independent clauses are sometimes called main clauses.

Example: "I'm going to back up my computer because it might crash." The independent clause is "I'm going to back up my computer" while the subordinate clause is "because it might crash."

**Indirect object**

An indirect object (of a verb) precedes the direct object and usually tells to whom or for whom the action of that verb is done.

Example: "The maître d' gave us a complimentary bottle of wine." The word "us" functions as the indirect object, even though it comes before the direct object. The words "bottle of wine" serve as the direct object.

See also Direct Object.

| | |
|---|---|
| **Infinitive** | Infinitives are verb forms, in which the basic form of a verb is preceded by "to." Infinitives generally function as nouns but may also function as adjectives or adverbs. Informally they may be referred to as word pairings in which the preposition "to" is placed in front of a verb. |
| | Examples: "To see is to believe." Note that "to see" and "to believe" are both infinitives. |
| **Interrogative pronoun** | Interrogative pronouns are used in questions. |
| | Examples: *who, which, what, whom,* and *whose.* |
| **Intransitive verb** | Intransitive verbs do not require an object to complete their meaning. |
| | Example: "He waits." The verb "waits" does not require an object to complete its meaning. |
| | See also Transitive Verb. |
| **Nonrestrictive clause** | A nonrestrictive clause is a clause that is not essential to the meaning of a sentence. Nonrestrictive clauses are generally enclosed by commas. |
| | Example: "The green book, which is on the top shelf, is the one you need for math class." "Which is on the top shelf" is a nonrestrictive clause. |

NOTE ❧ In choosing between "that" or "which," it is common practice to use "that" with restrictive (essential) phrases and clauses and "which" with nonrestrictive (nonessential) phrases and clauses. For this reason, "that" is used with clauses that are not set off by commas and to use "which" is used with clauses that are set off by commas.

See also Restrictive Clauses.

**Object**

An object (of a verb) is a word or words that receives the action of a verb. An object is a special kind of complement. Objects can be either direct objects or indirect objects.

See Direct Object and Indirect Object.

**Parenthetical expression**

Parenthetical expressions are expressions which are set off by commas and which seek to add some clarity to a sentence.

Example: "Yogurt, on the other hand, is a fine substitute for ice-cream." "On the other hand" is a parenthetical expression and could be removed from the sentence without destroying sentence meaning.

Words commonly used as parenthetical expressions include: *after all, by the way, for example, however, incidentally, indeed, in fact, in my opinion, naturally, nevertheless, of course, on the contrary, on the other hand, to tell you the truth.*

**Participle**

A participle is a verb form (ending in "ed" or "ing") that can function as an adjective. A participle is a type of verbal. Refer to the definition of "verbal."

Examples: "Cars parked near emergency exits will be towed." ("Parked" is a participle; it's an adjective describing "cars." The actual verb in the sentence is "will be towed.") "A sleeping dog never bit anyone." (The participle "sleeping" describes "dog." The actual verb in the sentence is "bit.")

**Participle phrase**

A participle phrase (also called a participial phrase) is a group of related words that contains a participle and, as a unit, typically functions as an adjective.

Examples: "Allowing plenty of time, Bill started studying twelve weeks before taking his College Board exams." "Allowing plenty of time" functions as a participle phrase in describing "Bill."

**Personal pronoun**

A personal pronoun is a pronoun designating the person speaking, the person spoken to, or the person or thing spoken about.

The following is a complete list of personal pronouns: *I, he, her, him, his, it, its, me, mine, my, our, ours, she, their, theirs, them, they, us, we, who, whom, whose, you, your, yours.*

**Phrase**

A phrase is a group of words which doesn't contain both a subject and a verb.

Examples: "Learning to be happy is difficult for a variety of reasons." The phrase "for a variety of reasons" does not contain a verb.

**Predicate**

A predicate is one of the two principal parts of a sentence. The predicate is "any word or words that talk about the subject"; the subject is "the word or words being talked about." Technically, the word "predicate" is a broader term than the word "verb," referring to both a verb and its possible complement. It is, however, much more common to refer to the *verb* and *complement* separately. In such cases, the *verb* can be referred to as the *simple predicate*; the *predicate* is referred to as the *complete predicate*.

Examples: "Water is the key to our survival." In this sentence, the subject is "water" and the predicate is "is the key to our survival." Breaking things down further, the predicate consists of the verb "is" and the complement "the key to our survival."

**Reflexive pronoun**

A reflexive pronoun refers back to a given noun or pronoun.

The following is a complete list of reflexive pronouns: *herself, himself, itself, myself, ourselves, themselves, yourself.*

**Relative clause**

A relative clause is a group of related words that begins with a relative pronoun, and as a unit, functions as an adjective. A relative clause is commonly referred to as an adjective clause (and sometimes as a subordinate adjective clause).

Examples: "Jim Thompson, who mysteriously disappeared while going for an afternoon walk on Easter Sunday, is credited with having revitalized the silk trade in Thailand." "Who mysteriously disappeared while going for an afternoon walk on Easter Sunday" is a relative clause which serves to modify "Jim Thompson."

See also Adjective Clause and Subordinate Clause.

**Relative pronoun**

A relative pronoun modifies a noun or pronoun (called its antecedent). A relative pronoun also begins a relative clause (also known as a subordinate adjective clause).

Examples: There are five relative pronouns in English: *that, which, who, whom,* and *whose.*

**Restrictive clause**

A restrictive clause is essential to the meaning of a sentence. Restrictive clauses are not enclosed by commas.

Example: "The book that is red is the one you need for English class." "That is red" is a restrictive clause.

**Run-on sentence**

A run-on sentence refers to two sentences that are inappropriately joined together, usually by a comma.

Example: "The weather is great, I'm going to the beach." (A comma cannot join two complete sentences. See *Appendix III – Punctuation Highlights* for further discussion on how to fix a run-on sentence).

**Sentence**

A sentence is a group of words that contains a subject and a verb, and can stand on its own as a complete thought.

Example: "The world is a stage." The subject is "the world" while the verb is "is"; the complete thought involves comparing the world to a stage.

**Sentence fragment**

A sentence fragment is a group of words that cannot stand on their own to form a complete thought.

Example: "A fine day." This statement is a fragment. It does not constitute a complete thought and cannot stand on its own. The fragment can be turned into a sentence by adding a subject ("today") and a verb ("is")—"Today is a fine day."

Sentence fragments are not acceptable for use in formal writing. In contrast, sentence fragments are commonly used in informal writing situations (e.g., e-mail and text messaging), and frequently seen in creative communications such as advertising, fiction writing, and poetry.

The following sentence fragments would be acceptable in informal written communication:

Will Michael Phelps' feat of eight gold medals in a single Olympics ever be equaled? <u>Never.</u>

We need to bring education to the world. <u>But how?</u>

<u>Dream on!</u> No one beats Brazil at football when its star forwards show up to play.

| | |
|---|---|
| **Split infinitive** | A split infinitive occurs when a word (usually an adverb) is placed between the two words that create an infinitive (i.e., between the word "to" and its accompanying verb). Splitting an infinitive is still considered a substandard practice in formal writing. |

Example: The sentence, "To boldly go where no one has gone before," contains a split infinitive. The sentence should be rewritten, "To go boldly where no one has gone before."

| | |
|---|---|
| **Subordinate clause** | A subordinate clause is a clause that cannot stand on its own as a complete sentence. It must instead be combined with at least one independent clause to form a complete sentence. Subordinate clauses are sometimes called dependent clauses. |

Example: "We should support the winning candidate whomever that may be." The subordinate clause is "whomever that may be." The independent clause is, "We should support the winning candidate."

**Subordinating conjunction**

A subordinating conjunction is a conjunction that begins an adverb clause and serves to join that clause to the rest of the sentence.

Examples: *after, although, as, as if, as long as, as though, because, before, if, in order that, provided that, since, so that, than, though, unless, until, when, whenever, where, wherever, whether, while.*

Note that many of the words in the above list, when used in different contexts, may also function as other parts of speech.

**Transitive verb**

Transitive verbs require an object to complete its meaning.

Example: "She posted a parcel." The verb "posted" requires an object, in this case "parcel," to complete its meaning.

See also Intransitive Verb.

**Verbal**

A verbal is a verb form that functions as a noun, adjective, or adverb. There are three types of verbals: gerunds, infinitives, and participles. Gerunds, infinitives, and participles can form phrases, in which case they are referred to as gerund phrases, infinitive phrases, and participle phrases.

# Word Gremlins

Diction, sometimes called "word usage," is about word choice. A writer often must choose between two similar words or expressions. The good news is that a small amount of concentrated study can greatly improve anyone's grasp of diction. The bad news is that most diction errors will not be picked up by a spell checker or grammar checker. Rather, they lurk in material until discovered and culled.

Idioms, herein referred to as grammatical idioms, are words and expressions that have become accepted due to the passage of time. They are right simply because "they're right." Even native speakers have trouble relying entirely on what sounds right. Fortunately, the compiled list of 200 common grammatical idioms will provide a welcome reference for preview and review.

## Diction Showdown

### Affect, Effect

*Affect* is a verb meaning "to influence." *Effect* is a noun meaning "result." *Effect* is also a verb meaning "to bring about."

The change in company policy will not <u>affect</u> our pay.

The long-term <u>effect</u> of space travel is not yet known.

A good mentor seeks to <u>effect</u> positive change.

### Afterward, Afterwards

These words are interchangeable: *afterward* is more commonly used in America while *afterwards* is more commonly used in Britain. A given written document should show consistent treatment.

### Allot, Alot, A lot

*Allot* is a verb meaning "to distribute" or "to apportion." *Alot* is not a word in the English language, but a common misspelling. *A lot* means "many."

To become proficient at yoga one must <u>allot</u> twenty minutes a day to practice.

Having <u>a lot</u> of free time is always a luxury.

### All ready, Already

*All ready* means "entirely ready" or "prepared." *Already* means "before or previously," but may also mean "now or soon."

Contingency plans ensure we are <u>all ready</u> in case the unexpected happens. (entirely ready or prepared)

We've <u>already</u> tried the newest brand. (before or previously)

Is it lunchtime <u>already</u>? (now or so soon)

## All together, Altogether

*All together* means "in one group." *Altogether* has two meanings. It can mean "completely," "wholly," or "entirely." It can also mean "in total."

Those going camping must be <u>all together</u> before they can board the bus.

The recommendation is <u>altogether</u> wrong.

There are six rooms <u>altogether</u>.

*NOTE* ⇜ The phrase "putting it all together" (four words) is correct. It means "putting it all in one place." The phrase "putting it altogether" (three words) is incorrect because it would effectively mean "putting it completely" or "putting it in total."

## Among, Amongst

These words are interchangeable: *among* is American English while *amongst* is British English. A given written document should show consistent treatment.

## Anymore, Any more

These words are not interchangeable. *Anymore* means "from this point forward." *Any more* refers to an unspecified additional amount.

I'm not going to dwell on this mishap <u>anymore</u>.

Are there <u>any more</u> tickets left?

## Anyone, Any one

These words are not interchangeable. *Anyone* means "any person" whereas *any one* means "any single person, item, or thing."

<u>Anyone</u> can take the exam.

<u>Any one</u> of these green vegetables is good for you.

## Anytime, Any time

These words are not necessarily interchangeable. *Anytime* is best thought of as an adverb which refers to "an unspecified period of time." *Any time* is an adjective-noun combination which means "an amount of time." Also, *any time* is always written as two words when it is preceded by the preposition "at"; in that case, its meaning is the same as its single word compatriot.

Call me <u>anytime</u> and we'll do lunch.

This weekend, I won't have <u>any time</u> to tweet (twitter).

At <u>any time</u> of the day, you can hear traffic if your window is open.

## Anyway, Any way

These words are not interchangeable. *Anyway* means "nevertheless, no matter what the situation is" or "in any case, no matter what." *Any way* means "any method or means."

Keep the printer. I wasn't using it <u>anyway</u>.

Is there <u>any way</u> of salvaging this umbrella?

*NOTE* ⤺ The word "anyways," previously considered nonstandard, is now considered an acceptable variant of "anyway," according to the *Merriam-Webster Collegiate Dictionary*.

## Apart, A part

These words are not interchangeable. *Apart* means "in separate pieces." *A part* means "a single piece or component."

Overhaul the machine by first taking it <u>apart</u>.

Every childhood memory is <u>a part</u> of our collective memory.

## Awhile, A while

These words are not interchangeable. *Awhile* is an adverb meaning "for a short time." *A while* is a noun phrase meaning "some time" and is usually preceded by "for."

Let's wait <u>awhile</u>.

I'm going to be gone for <u>a while</u>.

*NOTE* ✒ It is not correct to write: "Let's wait for awhile."

## As, Because, Since

These three words, when used as a conjunction meaning "for the reason that," are all interchangeable.

<u>As</u> everyone knows how to swim, let's go snorkeling.

<u>Because</u> all the youngsters had fishing rods, they went fishing.

<u>Since</u> we have firewood, we'll make a bonfire.

## Assure, Ensure, Insure

*Assure* is to inform positively. *Insure* is to arrange for financial payment in the case of loss. Both *ensure* and *insure* are now largely interchangeable in the sense of "to make certain." *Ensure,* however, implies a kind of virtual guarantee. *Insure* implies the taking of precautionary or preventative measures.

Don't worry. I <u>assure</u> you I'll be there by 8 a.m.

When shipping valuable antiques, a sender must <u>insure</u> any piece for its market value in the event it's damaged or lost.

Hard work is the best way to <u>ensure</u> success regardless of the endeavor.

Every large jewelry shop maintains an on-site safe to <u>insure</u> that inventory is secure during closing hours. (taking of precautionary measures)

## Because of, Due to, Owing to

These word pairings are interchangeable and mean "as a result of."

The climate is warming <u>because of</u> fossil fuel emissions.

Fossil fuel emissions are increasing <u>due to</u> industrialization.

<u>Owing to</u> global warming, the weather is less predictable.

## Better, Best

*Better* is used when comparing two things. *Best* is used when comparing three or more things.

Comparing Dan with Joe, Joe is the <u>better</u> cyclist.

Tina is the <u>best</u> student in the class.

## Between, Among

Use *between* to discuss two things. Use *among* to discuss three or more things.

The jackpot was divided <u>between</u> two winners.

Five plaintiffs were <u>among</u> the recipients of a cash settlement.

## Cannot, Can not

These words are interchangeable with "cannot" being by far the most popular written expression in both American and British English.

## Choose, Choosing, Chose, Chosen

*Choose* is present tense of the verb (rhymes with "blues"). *Choosing* is the present participle (rhymes with "cruising"). *Chose* is the past tense (rhymes with "blows"). *Chosen* is the past participle.

My plan was to <u>choose</u> blue or green for my company logo.

I ended up <u>choosing</u> teal, which is a blend of both colors.

Actually, we first <u>chose</u> turquoise but, soon after, realized that the shade we had <u>chosen</u> was a bit too bright.

*NOTE* ✄ There is no such word as "chosing." This word is sometimes mistaken for, and incorrectly used in place of, the present participle "choosing."

## Complement, Compliment

Both complement or compliment can be used as nouns or verbs. As a verb, *complement* means "to fill in," "to complete," or "to add to and make better"; as a noun it means "something that completes" or "something that improves." *Compliment* is used in two related ways. It is either "an expression of praise" (noun) or is used "to express praise" (verb).

A visit to the Greek islands is a perfect <u>complement</u> to any tour of bustling Athens. Visitors to the Greek island of Mykonos, for instance, are always struck by how the blue ocean <u>complements</u> the white, coastal buildings.

Throughout the awards ceremony, winners and runner-ups received <u>compliments</u> on a job well done. At closing, it was the attendees that <u>complimented</u> the organizers on a terrific event.

## Complementary, Complimentary

Both words are used as adjectives. Like complement, *complementary* means "to make complete," "to enhance," or "to improve" (e.g., complementary plans). *Complimentary* means "to praise" (e.g., complementary remarks) or "to receive or supply free of charge."

Only one thing is certain in the world of haute couture: fashion parties brimming with <u>complimentary</u> Champagne and endless banter on how colorful characters and <u>complementary</u> personalities rose to the occasion.

## Differs from, Differ with

Use *differ from* in discussing characteristics. Use *differ with* to convey the idea of disagreement.

American English <u>differs from</u> British English.

The clerk <u>differs with</u> her manager on his decision to hire an additional salesperson.

## Different from, Different than

These two word pairings are interchangeable. However, whereas *different from* is used to compare two nouns or phases, *different than* is commonly used when what follows is a clause.

Dolphins are <u>different from</u> porpoises.

My old neighborhood is <u>different than</u> it used to be.

## Do to, Due to

*Do to* consists of the verb "do" followed by the preposition "to." *Due to* is an adverbial phrase meaning "because of" or "owing to." *Due to* is sometimes erroneously written as *do to*.

What can we <u>do to</u> save the mountain gorilla?

Roads are slippery <u>due to</u> heavy rain.

## Each other, One another

Use *each other* when referring to two people. Use *one another* when referring to more than two people.

Two weight lifters helped spot <u>each other</u>.

Olympic athletes compete against <u>one another</u>.

## Everyday, Every day

These words are not interchangeable. *Everyday* is an adjective that means either "ordinary" or "unremarkable" (everyday chores) or happening each day (an everyday occurrence). *Every day* is an adverb meaning "each day" or "every single day."

Although we're fond of talking about the <u>everyday</u> person, it's difficult to know what this really means.

Health practitioners say we should eat fresh fruit <u>every day</u>.

## Everyplace, Every place

These words are not interchangeable. *Everyplace* has the same meaning as "everywhere." *Every place* means in "each space" or "each spot."

We looked <u>everyplace</u> for that DVD.

<u>Every place</u> was taken by the time she arrived.

## Everyone, Every one

These words are not interchangeable. *Everyone* means "everybody in a group" whereas *every one* means "each person."

Everyone knows who did it!

Every one of the runners who crossed the finish line was exhausted but jubilant.

## Everything, Every thing

*Everything* means "all things." *Every thing* means "each thing." Note that the word *everything* is much more common than its two-word counterpart.

Everything in this store is on sale.

Just because we don't understand the role that each living organism plays, this doesn't mean that to every thing there isn't a purpose.

## Every time, Everytime

*Every time* means "at any and all times." It is always spelled as two separate words. Spelling it as one word is nonstandard and incorrect.

Every time we visit there's always lots of food and drink.

## Farther, Further

Use *farther* when referring to distance. Use *further* in all other situations, particularly when referring to extent or degree.

The town is one mile farther along the road.

We must pursue this idea further.

## Fewer, Less

*Fewer* refers to things that can be counted, e.g., people, marbles, accidents. *Less* refers to things that cannot be counted, e.g., money, water, sand.

There are <u>fewer</u> students in class than before the midterm exam.

There is <u>less</u> water in the bucket due to evaporation.

## If, Whether

Use *if* to express one possibility, especially conditional statements. Use *whether* to express two (or more) possibilities.

The company claims that you will be successful <u>if</u> you listen to their tapes on motivation.

Success depends on <u>whether</u> one has desire and determination. (The implied "whether or not" creates two possibilities.)

*NOTE* ॐ In colloquial English, *if* and *whether* are now interchangeable. Either of the following sentences would be correct: "I'm not sure <u>whether</u> I'm going to the party."/"I'm not sure <u>if</u> I'm going to the party."

## Instead of, Rather than

These word pairs are considered interchangeable.

Lisa ordered Rocky Road ice cream <u>instead of</u> Mint Chocolate.

The customer wanted a refund <u>rather than</u> an exchange.

## Infer, Imply

*Infer* means "to draw a conclusion"; readers or listeners infer. *Imply* means "to hint" or to suggest"; speakers or writers imply.

I <u>infer</u> from your letter that conditions have improved.

Do you mean to <u>imply</u> that conditions have improved?

## Into, In to

These words are not interchangeable. *Into* means "something inside something else." The phrase *in to* means "something is passing from one place to another."

The last I saw she was walking <u>into</u> the cafeteria.

He finally turned his assignment <u>in to</u> the teacher.

Regarding the sentence above, unless the student were a magician, we could not write, "He finally turned his assignment *into* the teacher."

## Its, It's

*Its* is a possessive pronoun. *It's* is a contraction for "it is" or "it has."

The world has lost <u>its</u> glory.

<u>It's</u> time to start anew.

## Lead, Led

The verb *lead* means "to guide, direct, command, or cause to follow." *Lead* is the present tense of the verb while *led* forms the past tense (and past participle).

More than any other player, the captain is expected to <u>lead</u> his team during the playoffs. Last season, however, it was our goalie, not the captain, who actually <u>led</u> our team to victory.

It is a common mistake to write "lead," when what is called for is "led." This error likely arises given that the irregular verb "read" is spelled the same in the present tense and in the past tense. Example: "I <u>read</u> the newspaper everyday, and yesterday, I <u>read</u> an amazing story about a 'tree' man whose arms and legs resembled bark."

## Lets, Let's

*Lets* is a verb meaning "to allow or permit." *Let's* is a contraction for "let us."

Technology <u>lets</u> us live more easily.

<u>Let's</u> not forget those who fight for our liberties.

## Lie, Lay

In the present tense, *lie* means "to rest" and *lay* means "to put" or "to place." Lie is an intransitive verb (a verb that does not require a direct object to complete its meaning), while lay is a transitive verb (a verb that requires a direct object to complete its meaning).

Lie

| | |
|---|---|
| *Present* | <u>Lie</u> on the sofa. |
| *Past* | He <u>lay</u> down for an hour. |
| *Perfect Participle* | He <u>has lain</u> there for an hour. |
| *Present Participle* | It was nearly noon and he was still <u>lying</u> on the sofa. |

Lay

| | |
|---|---|
| *Present* | <u>Lay</u> the magazine on the table. |
| *Past* | She <u>laid</u> the magazine there yesterday. |
| *Perfect Participle* | She <u>has laid</u> the magazine there many times. |
| *Present Participle* | <u>Laying</u> the magazine on the table, she stood up and left the room. |

*NOTE* ∽ There is no such word as "layed." This word is the mistaken misspelling of "laid." Example: "A magazine cover that is professionally laid out," not "a magazine cover that is professionally layed out."

## Like, Such as

*Such as* is used for listing items in a series. *Like* should not be used for listing items in a series. However, *like* is okay to use when introducing a single item.

A beginning rugby player must master many different skills <u>such as</u> running and passing, blocking and tackling, drop kicking, and scrum control.

Dark fruits, <u>like</u> beets, have an especially good cleansing quality.

## Loose, Lose, Loss

*Loose* is an adjective meaning "not firmly attached" or "not tightly drawn." *Lose* is a verb meaning "to suffer a setback or deprivation." *Loss* is a noun meaning "a failure to achieve."

A <u>loose</u> screw will fall out if not tightened.

There is some truth to the idea that if you're going to <u>lose</u>, you might as well <u>lose</u> big.

<u>Loss</u> of habitat is a greater threat to wildlife conservation than is poaching.

## Maybe, May be

These words are not interchangeable. *Maybe* is an adverb meaning "perhaps." *May be* is a verb phrase.

<u>Maybe</u> it's time to try again.

It <u>may be</u> necessary to resort to extreme measures.

## Might, May

Although *might* and *may* both express a degree of uncertainty, they have somewhat different meanings. *Might* expresses more uncertainty than does *may*. Also, only *might* is the correct choice when referring to past situations.

I <u>might</u> like to visit the Taj Mahal someday. (much uncertainty)

I <u>may</u> go sightseeing this weekend. (less uncertainty)

They <u>might</u> have left a message for us at the hotel. (past situation)

## No one, Noone

*No one* means "no person." It should be spelled as two separate words. The one-word spelling is nonstandard and incorrect.

<u>No one</u> can predict the future.

## Number, Amount

Use *number* when speaking of things that can be counted. Use *amount* when speaking of things that cannot be counted.

The <u>number</u> of marbles in the bag is seven.

The <u>amount</u> of topsoil has eroded considerably.

## Onto, On to

These words are not equivalent. *Onto* refers to "something placed on something else." The phrase *on to* consists of the adverb "on" and the preposition "to."

Ferry passengers could be seen holding <u>onto</u> the safety rail.

We passed the information <u>on to</u> our friends.
Note that we could not pass the information *onto* our friends unless the information was placed physically on top of them.

## Passed, Past

*Passed* functions as a verb. *Past* functions as a noun, adjective, or preposition.

Yesterday, Cindy found out that she <u>passed</u> her much-feared anatomy exam.

The proactive mind does not dwell on events of the <u>past</u>.

## Principal, Principle

Although *principal* can refer to the head administrator of a school or even an original amount of money on loan, it is usually used as an adjective meaning "main," "primary," or "most important." *Principle* is used in one of two senses: to refer to a general scientific law or to describe a person's fundamental belief system.

Lack of clearly defined goals is the <u>principal</u> cause of failure.

To be a physicist one must clearly understand the <u>principles</u> of mathematics.

A person of <u>principle</u> lives by a moral code.

## Sometime, Some time

These words are not interchangeable. *Sometime* refers to "an unspecified, often longer period of time." *Some time* refers to "a specified, often shorter period of time."

Let's have lunch <u>sometime</u>.

We went fishing early in the morning, but it was <u>some time</u> before we landed our first trout.

## Than, Then

*Than* is a conjunction used in making comparisons. *Then* is an adverb indicating time.

There is controversy over whether the Petronas Towers in Malaysia is taller <u>than</u> the Sears Tower in Chicago.

Finish your work first, <u>then</u> give me a call.

## That, Which

The words *which* and *that* mean essentially the same thing. But in context they are used differently. It is common practice to use *which* with nonrestrictive (nonessential) phrases and clauses and to use *that* with restrictive (essential) phrases and clauses. Nonrestrictive phrases are typically enclosed with commas, whereas restrictive phrases are never enclosed with commas. This treatment means that *which* appears in phrases set off by commas whereas *that* does not appear in phrases set off by commas.

The insect <u>that</u> has the shortest lifespan is the Mayfly.

The Mayfly, <u>which</u> lives less than 24 hours, has the shortest lifespan of any insect.

## That, Which, Who

In general, *who* is used to refer to people, *which* is used to refer to things, and *that* can refer to either people or things. When referring to people, the choice between *that* and *who* should be based on what feels more natural.

Choose a person <u>that</u> can take charge.

The person <u>who</u> is most likely to succeed is often not an obvious choice.

*NOTE* ⤢ On occasion, *who* is used to refer to non-persons while *which* may refer to people.

I have a dog <u>who</u> is animated and has a great personality.

<u>Which</u> child won the award? (The pronoun *which* is used to refer to a person.)

## There, Their, They're

*There* is an adverb. *Their* is a possessive pronoun. *They're* is a contraction for "they are."

<u>There</u> is a rugby game tonight.

<u>Their</u> new TV has incredibly clear definition.

<u>They're</u> a strange but happy couple.

## Toward, Towards

These words are interchangeable: *toward* is American English while *towards* is British English. A given written document should show consistent treatment.

## Used to, Use to

These words are not interchangeable. *Used to* is the correct form for habitual action. However, when "did" precedes "used to" the correct form is *use to*.

I used to go to the movies all the time.

I didn't use to daydream.

## Who, Whom

"Who" is the subjective form of the pronoun and "whom" is the objective form. The following is a good rule in deciding between *who* and *whom:* If "he, she, or they" can be substituted for a pronoun in context, the correct form is *who.* If "him, her, or them" can be substituted for a pronoun in context, the correct form is *whom.* Another very useful rule is that pronouns take their objective forms when they are the direct objects of prepositions.

Let's reward the person who can find the best solution.

Test: "He" or "she" can find the best solution, so the subjective form of the pronoun—"who"—is correct.

The report was compiled by whom?

Test: This report was drafted by "him" or "her," so the objective form of the pronoun—"whom"—is correct. Another way of confirming this is to note that "whom" functions as the direct object of the preposition "by," so the objective form of the pronoun is correct.

NOTE ❧ One particularly tricky situation occurs in the following: "She asked to speak to <u>whoever</u> was on duty." At first glance, it looks as though "whomever" should be correct in so far as "who" appears to be the object of the preposition "to." However, the whole clause "whoever was on duty" is functioning as the direct object of the preposition "to." The key is to analyze the function of "whoever" within the applicable clause itself; in this case, "whoever" is functioning as the subject of the verb "was," thereby taking the subjective form. We can test this by saying "*he* or *she* was on duty."

Let's analyze two more situations, each introduced by a sentence that contains correct usage.

1) "I will interview <u>whomever</u> I can find for the job." The important thing is to analyze the role of "whomever" within the clause "whomever I can find" and test it as "I can find *him* or *her*." This confirms that the objective form of the pronoun is correct. In this instance, the whole clause "whomever I can find" is modifying the verb form "will interview."

2) "I will give the position to <u>whoever</u> I think is right for the job." Again, the critical thing is to analyze the role of "whoever" within the clause "whoever I think is right for the job." Since we can say "I think he or she is right for the job," this confirms that the subjective form of the pronoun is correct. In this instance, the whole clause "whoever I think is right for the job" is modifying the preposition "to." Therefore, this example mirrors the previous example, "She asked to speak to <u>whoever</u> was on duty."

## Whose, Who's

*Whose* is a possessive pronoun. *Who's* is a contraction for "who is."

<u>Whose</u> set of keys did I find?

He is the player <u>who's</u> most likely to make the NBA.

## Your, You're

*Your* is a possessive pronoun. *You're* is a contraction for "you are."

This is <u>your</u> book.

<u>You're</u> becoming the person you want to be.

## 200 Common Grammatical Idioms

### ABC

1.     able to X
2.     account for
3.     according to
4.     a craving for
5.     a debate over
6.     a descendant of
7.     affiliated with
8.     agree to (a plan or action)
9.     agree with (person/idea)
10.     allow(s) for
11.     amount to
12.     a native of
13.     angry at/angry with
14.     appeal to
15.     apply to/apply for
16.     approve(d) of/disapprove(d) of
17.     a responsibility to
18.     argue with/over
19.     a sequence of
20.     as a consequence of X
21.     as … as
22.     as … as do/as … as does
23.     as a result of
24.     as good as
25.     as good as or better than
26.     as great as
27.     as many X as Y
28.     as much as
29.     as X is to Y
30.     ask X to do Y
31.     associate with
32.     attempt to
33.     attend to
34.     attest to

35.  attribute X to Y
36.  assure that
37.  averse to
38.  based on
39.  be afraid of
40.  because of
41.  believe X to be Y
42.  better served by X than by Y
43.  better than
44.  between X and Y
45.  both X and Y
46.  capable of
47.  centers on
48.  choice of
49.  choose from/choose to
50.  claim to be
51.  collaborate with
52.  compare to/compare with
53.  comply with
54.  composed of
55.  concerned about/with (not "concerned at")
56.  conform to
57.  conclude that
58.  connection between X and Y
59.  consider(ed) (without "to be")
60.  consider(ed) (with "to be")
61.  consistent with
62.  contend that
63.  contrast X with Y
64.  convert to
65.  cost of/cost to
66.  credit(ed) X with having

**DEF**

67.  debate over
68.  decide on/decide to
69.  declare X to be Y

70. defend against
71. define(d) as
72. delighted by
73. demand that
74. demonstrate that
75. depend(ent) on
76. depends on whether
77. depict(ed) as
78. descend(ed) from
79. desirous of
80. determined by
81. differ from/differ with
82. different from
83. difficult to
84. disagree with (person/idea)
85. discourage from
86. differentiate between X and Y
87. differentiate X from Y
88. dispute whether
89. distinguish X from Y
90. divergent from
91. do so/doing so (not "do it"/"doing it")
92. doubt that
93. draw on
94. either X or Y
95. enable X to Y
96. enamored of/with
97. enough X that Y
98. estimated to be
99. expect to
100. expose(d) to
101. fascinated by
102. fluctuations in
103. forbid X and Y
104. frequency of
105. from X rather than from Y (not "from X instead of Y")
106. from X to Y

## GHI

| 107. | give credit for/give credit to |
|------|--------------------------------|
| 108. | hypothesize that |
| 109. | in an effort to |
| 110. | in association with |
| 111. | indifferent toward(s) |
| 112. | infected with |
| 113. | inherit X from Y |
| 114. | in order to |
| 115. | in reference to/with reference to |
| 116. | in regard to/with regard to |
| 117. | in search of |
| 118. | insists that |
| 119. | intend(ed) to |
| 120. | intersection of X and Y |
| 121. | in the same way as ... to |
| 122. | in the same way that |
| 123. | introduce(d) to |
| 124. | in violation of |
| 125. | isolate(d) from |

## JKL

| 126. | just as X, so (too) Y |
|------|-----------------------|
| 127. | less X than Y |
| 128. | likely to/likely to be |
| 129. | liken to |

## MNO

| 130. | meet with |
|------|-----------|
| 131. | mistake (mistook) X for Y |
| 132. | model(ed) after |
| 133. | more common among X than among Y |
| 134. | more ... than ever |
| 135. | more X than Y |
| 136. | native to |

137. neither X nor Y
138. no less ... than
139. no less was X than was Y
140. not X but rather Y
141. not only X but (also) Y
142. not so much X as Y
143. on account of
144. on the one hand/on the other hand

## PQR

145. opposed to/opposition to
146. opposite of
147. inclined to
148. in comparison to
149. in conjunction with
150. in contrast to
151. in danger of
152. independent from
153. owing to
154. persuade X to Y
155. partake (partook) of
156. permit X to Y
157. potential to
158. prefer X to Y (not "prefer X over Y")
159. preferable to
160. prejudiced against
161. prevent from
162. prized by
163. prohibit X from Y
164. protect against
165. question whether
166. range(s) from X to Y
167. rates for (not "rates of")
168. recover from X
169. recover X from Y
170. regard(ed) as
171. replace(d) with

172. responsible for
173. resulting in

## STU

174. sacrifice X for Y
175. seem to indicate
176. similar to
177. so as not to be hindered by
178. so X as to be Y
179. so X as to constitute Y
180. so X that Y
181. subscribe to
182. such X as Y and Z
183. sympathy for
184. sympathize with
185. tamper with
186. targeted at
187. the more X the greater Y
188. the same to X as to Y
189. to result in
190. to think of X as Y
191. tying X to Y
192. used to (not "use to")

## VWXZY

193. view X as Y
194. whether X or Y
195. worry about (not "over")
196. X enough to Y
197. X instead of Y
198. X is attributed to Y
199. X out of Y (numbers)
200. X regarded as Y

# 30-All Star Grammar Problems

These thirty all-star grammar problems are grouped according to the "big six" grammar categories as introduced in the *100-Question Quiz*. Although grammar is the driving force behind each problem, issues relating to diction or idioms may be interwoven subcomponents. Read each question, deciding whether the underlined portion of each sentence needs to be changed to yield the *best* answer. If you feel the original sentence reads best among the choices, choose choice A, which is merely a restatement of the original; otherwise choose one of the variant answers B through E.

In addition to the answers and explanations included at the end of this section, each problem has a *Skill Rating*—easy (✻), medium (✻✻), or difficult (✻✻✻)—as well as a *Snapshot* caption to briefly explain why a given problem was chosen.

## 30 All-Star Grammar Problems

*Subject-Verb Agreement:*

### 1. Vacation (✷)

Neither Martha or her sisters are going on vacation.

A)    Neither Martha or her sisters are going on vacation.

B)    Neither Martha or her sisters is going on vacation.

C)    Neither any of her sisters nor Martha are going on vacation.

D)    Neither Martha nor her sisters are going on vacation.

E)    Neither Martha nor her sisters is going on vacation.

### 2. Leader (✷)

The activities of our current leader have led to a significant increase in the number of issues relating to the role of the military in non-military, nation-building exercises.

A)    have led to a significant increase in the number of issues relating to the role of the military in non-military, nation-building exercises.

B)    have been significant in the increase in the amount of issues relating to the role of the military in non-military, nation-building exercises.

C)    has led to a significant increase in the number of issues relating to the role of the military in non-military, nation-building exercises.

D) has been significant in the increase in the number of issues relating to the role of the military in non-military, nation-building exercises.

E) has significantly increased the amount of issues relating to the role of the military in non-military, nation-building exercises.

## 3. Marsupial (✶✶)

According to scientists at the University of California, the pattern of changes that have occurred in placental DNA over the millennia <u>indicate the possibility that every marsupial alive today might be descended from a single female ancestor that</u> lived in Africa sometime between 125 and 150 million years ago.

A) indicate the possibility that every marsupial alive today might be descended from a single female ancestor that

B) indicate that every marsupial alive today might possibly be a descendant of a single female ancestor that had

C) may indicate that every marsupial alive today has descended from a single female ancestor that had

D) indicates that every marsupial alive today might be a descendant of a single female ancestor that

E) indicates that every marsupial alive today may be a descendant from a single female ancestor that

### 4. Critics' Choice (✷✷)

<u>In this critically acclaimed film, there are a well-developed plot and an excellent cast of characters.</u>

A) In this critically acclaimed film, there are a well-developed plot and an excellent cast of characters.

B) In this critically acclaimed film, there is a well-developed plot and an excellent cast of characters.

C) In this film, which is critically acclaimed, there is a well-developed plot and an excellent cast of characters.

D) In this film, which has been critically acclaimed, there are a well-developed plot and an excellent cast of characters.

E) There is a well-developed plot and an excellent cast of characters in this critically acclaimed film.

### 5. Recommendations (✷✷)

<u>Implementing the consultants' recommendations is expected to result in</u> both increased productivity and decreased costs.

A) Implementing the consultants' recommendations is expected to result in

B) Implementing the consultants' recommendations are expected to result in

C) The expected result of enacting the consultants' recommendations are

D) The expected results of enacting the consultants' recommendations is

E) It is expected that enactment of the consultants' recommendations are to result in

*Pronoun Usage:*

## 6. Valuation (✫✫✫)

Financial formulas for valuing companies do not apply to Internet companies in the same way as they do to traditional businesses, because they are growing and seldom have ascertainable sales and cash flows.

A) Financial formulas for valuing companies do not apply to Internet companies in the same way as they do to traditional businesses, because they are growing and seldom have ascertainable sales and cash flows.

B) Internet companies are not subject to the same applicability of financial formulas for valuing these companies as compared with traditional businesses, because they are growing and seldom have ascertainable sales and cash flows.

C) Because they are growing and seldom have ascertainable sales and cash flows, financial formulas for valuing companies do not apply to Internet companies in the same way as they do to traditional businesses.

D) Because they are growing and seldom have ascertainable sales and cash flows, Internet companies are not subject to the same applicability of financial valuation formulas as are traditional businesses.

E)     Because Internet companies are growing and
       seldom have ascertainable sales and cash flows,
       financial formulas for valuing these companies do
       not apply to them in the same way as to traditional
       businesses.

## 7. Inland Taipan (✳✳)

The Inland Taipan or Fierce Snake of central Australia is
widely <u>regarded to be the world's most venomous snake;
the poison from its bite can kill human victims unless
treated</u> within thirty minutes of an incident.

A)     regarded to be the world's most venomous snake;
       the poison from its bite can kill human victims
       unless treated

B)     regarded as the world's most venomous snake; the
       poison from its bite can kill human victims unless
       treated

C)     regarded to be the world's most venomous snake;
       the poison from its bite can kill human victims
       unless it is treated

D)     regarded as the world's most venomous snake; the
       poison from its bite can kill human victims unless
       they are treated

E)     regarded to be the world's most venomous snake;
       the poison from its bite can kill human victims
       unless they are treated

## 8. Medicare (✶)

Although Medicare legislation is being considered by
the House of Representatives, they do not expect it to
pass without being significantly revised.

A)  Although Medicare legislation is being considered
    by the House of Representatives, they do not
    expect it to pass without being significantly
    revised.

B)  Although the House of Representatives is
    considering Medicare legislation, they do not
    expect it to pass without significant revision.

C)  Although the House of Representatives is
    considering Medicare legislation, it is not expected
    to pass without being significantly revised.

D)  If it is to be passed, the House of Representatives
    must significantly revise Medicare legislation.

E)  Consideration and significant revision is expected
    if Medicare legislation is to be passed by the House
    of Representatives.

## 9. Oceans (✶)

One cannot gauge the immensity of the world's oceans
until you have tried to sail around the world.

A)  One cannot gauge the immensity of the world's
    oceans until you have tried to sail around the
    world.

B)  One cannot gauge the immensity of the world's
    oceans until they have tried to sail around the
    world.

C) One cannot gauge the immensity of the world's oceans until he or she has tried to sail around the world.

D) A person cannot gauge the immensity of the world's oceans until you have tried to sail around the world.

E) A person cannot gauge the immensity of the world's oceans until they have tried to sail around the world.

*Modification:*

## 10. Metal Detector (✶)

Using a metal detector, old coins and other valuables can be located by hobbyists even though they are buried in the sand and dirt.

A) Using a metal detector, old coins and other valuables can be located by hobbyists even though they are buried in the sand and dirt.

B) Old coins and other valuables can be located by hobbyists using a metal detector even though they are buried in the sand and dirt.

C) Using a metal detector, hobbyists can locate old coins and other valuables even though they are buried in the sand and dirt.

D) Buried in the sand and dirt, old coins and other valuables can be located by hobbyists using a metal detector.

E) A metal detector can be used to locate old coins and other valuables that are buried in the sand and dirt by a hobbyist.

## 11. Hungary (✶✶)

<u>With</u> less than one percent of the world's population, Hungarians have made disproportionately large contributions to the fields of modern math and applied science.

A)   With

B)   Having

C)   Despite having

D)   Although constituting

E)   In addition to accounting for

## 12. Natural Beauty (✶✶)

Plastic surgeons who perform surgery for non-medical reasons defend their practice on the basis of the free rights of their patients; many others in the health field, however, contend that plastic surgery degrades natural beauty, <u>which they liken to reconstructing a national park.</u>

A)   which they liken to reconstructing a national park.

B)   which they liken to a national park with reconstruction done to it.

C)   which they liken to reconstruction done on a national park.

D)   likening it to a national park with reconstruction done to it.

E)   likening it to reconstructing a national park.

*Parallelism:*

## 13. Cannelloni (✷)

<u>Cannelloni has and always will be my favorite Italian dish.</u>

A) Cannelloni has and always will be my favorite Italian dish.

B) Cannelloni was, has, and always will be my favorite Italian dish.

C) Cannelloni was and always will be my favorite Italian dish.

D) Cannelloni has been and always will be my favorite Italian dish.

E) Cannelloni is, has, and always will be my favorite Italian dish.

## 14. Massage (✷✷)

Massage creates a relaxing, therapeutic, and rejuvenating experience <u>both for your body and your well-being.</u>

A) both for your body and your well-being.

B) for both your body and your well-being.

C) both for your body and well-being.

D) for both your body and well-being.

E) both for your body as well as your well-being.

## 15. Europeans (✲✲✲)

Italy is famous for its composers and musicians, France, for its chefs and philosophers, and Poland, for its mathematicians and logicians.

A) Italy is famous for its composers and musicians, France, for its chefs and philosophers, and Poland, for its mathematicians and logicians.

B) Italy is famous for its composers and musicians, France for its chefs and philosophers, Poland for its mathematicians and logicians.

C) Italy is famous for its composers and musicians. France for its chefs and philosophers. Poland for its mathematicians and logicians.

D) Italy is famous for their composers and musicians; France, for their chefs and philosophers; Poland for their mathematicians and logicians.

E) Italy, France, and Poland are famous for their composers and musicians, chefs and philosophers, and mathematicians and logicians.

*Comparisons:*

## 16. Sweater (✲)

Although neither sweater is really the right size, the smallest one fits best.

A) the smallest one fits best.

B) the smallest one fits better.

C) the smallest one is better fitting.

D) the smaller of the two fits best.

E) the smaller one fits better.

## 17. Sir Isaac Newton (✻)

Within the scientific community, the accomplishments of Sir Isaac Newton are referred to more often <u>than any</u> scientist, living or dead.

A)   than any

B)   than any other

C)   than those of any

D)   than are those of any

E)   than those of any other

## 18. Soya (✻✻)

In addition to having more protein than meat does, <u>the protein in soybeans is higher in quality than that in meat.</u>

A)   the protein in soybeans is higher in quality than that in meat.

B)   the protein in soybeans is higher in quality than it is in meat.

C)   Soybeans have protein of higher quality than that in meat.

D)   Soybean protein is higher in quality than it is in meat.

E)   Soybeans have protein higher in quality than meat.

**19. Angel (✷✷)**

She sings like an angel sings.

A)    She sings like an angel sings.

B)    She sings like an angel does.

C)    She sings as an angel sings.

D)    She sings as if an angel.

E)    She sings as if like an angel.

**20. Perceptions (✷✷)**

Because right-brained individuals do not employ convergent thinking processes, like left-brained individuals, they may not notice and remember the same level of detail as their counterparts.

A)    like left-brained individuals,

B)    unlike a left-brained individual,

C)    as left-brained individuals,

D)    as left-brained individuals do,

E)    as a left-brained individual can,

## 21. Geography (✷✷)

Despite the fact that the United States is a superpower, <u>American high school students perform more poorly on tests of world geography and international affairs than do</u> their Canadian counterparts.

A) American high school students perform more poorly on tests of world geography and international affairs than do

B) American high school students perform more poorly on tests of world geography and international affairs as compared with

C) American high school students perform more poorly on tests of world geography and international affairs as compared to

D) the American high school student performs more poorly on tests of world geography and international affairs than does

E) the American high school student performs more poorly on tests of world geography and international affairs as compared with

## 22. Assemblée Nationale (✷✷)

<u>As Parliament is the legislative government body of Great Britain,</u> the Assemblée Nationale is the legislative government body of France.

A) As Parliament is the legislative government body of Great Britain,

B) As the legislative government body of Great Britain is Parliament,

C)   Just like the legislative government body of Great
     Britain, which is Parliament,

D)   Just as Parliament is the legislative government
     body of Great Britain, so

E)   Just as the government of Britain's legislative
     branch is Parliament,

**23. Bear (✷✷✷)**

Like the Alaskan brown bear and most other members
of the bear family, the diet of the grizzly bear consists of
both meat and vegetation.

A)   Like the Alaskan brown bear and most other
     members of the bear family, the diet of the grizzly
     bear consists

B)   Like those of the Alaskan brown bear and most
     other members of the bear family, the diets of a
     grizzly bear consist

C)   Like the Alaskan brown bear and most other
     members of the bear family, the grizzly bear has a
     diet consisting

D)   Just like the diet of the Alaskan brown bear and
     most other members of the bear family, the diets
     of the grizzly bear consist

E)   Similar to the diets of the Alaskan brown bear and
     most other members of the bear family, grizzly
     bears have a diet which consists

## 24. Smarts (✷✷✷)

Unlike the Miller Analogies Test, which follows a standardized format, <u>the formats for IQ tests vary considerably in both content and length.</u>

A) the formats for IQ tests vary considerably in both content and length.

B) the format for an IQ test varies considerably in both content and length.

C) an IQ test follows a format that varies considerably in both content and length.

D) an IQ test follows formats that vary considerably in both content and length.

E) IQ tests follow formats that vary considerably in both content and length.

*Verb Tenses:*

## 25. Golden Years (✷)

According to the findings of a recent study, many executives <u>had elected early retirement rather than face</u> the threats of job cuts and diminishing retirement benefits.

A) had elected early retirement rather than face

B) had elected to retire early rather than face

C) have elected early retirement instead of facing

D) have elected early retirement rather than facing

E) have elected to retire early rather than face

## 26. Politics (✩✩)

Although he <u>disapproved of the political platform set forth by Senator Barack Obama during the 2008 U.S. presidential primaries, Senator John McCain had later conceded</u> that there must be a basis for a coalition government and urged members of both parties to seek compromise.

A) disapproved of the political platform set forth by Senator Barack Obama during the 2008 U.S. presidential primaries, Senator John McCain had later conceded

B) has disapproved of the political platform set forth by Senator Barack Obama during the 2008 U.S. presidential primaries, Senator John McCain had later conceded

C) has disapproved of the political platform set forth by Senator Barack Obama during the 2008 U.S. presidential primaries, Senator John McCain later conceded

D) had disapproved of the political platform set forth by Senator Barack Obama during the 2008 U.S. presidential primaries, Senator John McCain later conceded

E) had disapproved of the political platform set forth by Senator Barack Obama during the 2008 U.S. presidential primaries, Senator John McCain had later conceded

## 27. Trend (★★)

The percentage of people remaining single in Holland
increased abruptly between 1980 and 1990 and continued
to rise more gradually over the next 10 years.

A) The percentage of people remaining single in
Holland increased abruptly between 1980 and
1990 and continued to rise more gradually over the
next ten years.

B) The percentage of people remaining single in
Holland increased abruptly between 1980 and
1990 and has continued to rise more gradually
over the next ten years.

C) The percentage of people remaining single in
Holland increased abruptly between 1980 and
1990 and had continued to rise more gradually
over the next ten years.

D) There had been an abrupt increase in the
percentage of people remaining single in Holland
between 1980 and 1990 and it continued to rise
more gradually over the next ten years.

E) There was an abrupt increase in the percentage of
people remaining single in Holland between 1980
and 1990 which continued to rise more gradually
over the next ten years.

**28. Fire (✷✷)**

<u>Most houses that were destroyed and heavily damaged in residential fires last year were</u> built without adequate fire detection apparatus.

A)   Most houses that were destroyed and heavily damaged in residential fires last year were

B)   Most houses that were destroyed or heavily damaged in residential fires last year had been

C)   Most houses that were destroyed and heavily damaged in residential fires last year had been

D)   Most houses that were destroyed or heavily damaged in residential fires last year have been

E)   Most houses that were destroyed and heavily damaged in residential fires last year have been

**29. B-School (✷✷)**

<u>As graduate management programs become more competitive in the coming years in terms of their promotional and financial undertakings, schools have been becoming</u> more and more dependent on alumni networks, corporate sponsorships, and philanthropists.

A)   As graduate management programs become more competitive in the coming years in terms of their promotional and financial undertakings, schools have been becoming

B)   As graduate management programs are becoming more competitive in the coming years in terms of their promotional and financial undertakings, schools have been becoming

C) As graduate management programs become more competitive in the coming years in terms of their promotional and financial undertakings, schools have become

D) As graduate management programs are becoming more competitive in the coming years in terms of their promotional and financial undertakings, schools have become

E) As graduate management programs become more competitive in the coming years in terms of their promotional and financial undertakings, schools will become

## 30. Summer in Europe (✲✲)

By the time we have reached France, we will have been backpacking for twelve weeks.

A) By the time we have reached France, we will have been backpacking for twelve weeks.

B) By the time we have reached France, we will have backpacked for twelve weeks.

C) By the time we reach France, we will have been backpacking for twelve weeks.

D) By the time we will have reached France, we will have backpacked for twelve weeks.

E) By the time we reached France, we will have been backpacking for twelve weeks.

## Answers and Explanations

### 1. Vacation (✳)

**Choice D**
**Classification:** Subject-Verb Agreement
**Skill Rating:** Easy
**Snapshot:** This problem is included to highlight the handling of correlative conjunctions, namely "either/or" and "neither/nor," which may involve the use of a singular or plural verb.

The consistent appearance of "neither" (in answer choices A through E) indicates a "neither...nor" relationship. We can eliminate choices A and B outright. The correct verb should match the noun that comes after the word "nor." Since "her sisters" in D is plural, the plural verb "are" does the trick.

In summary, singular subjects following "or" or "nor" always take a singular verb; plural subjects following "or" or "nor" take a plural verb. Stated another way, when two items are connected by "or" or "nor," the verb agrees with the closer subject. That is, the verb needs only agree with the subject that comes after "or" or "nor."

There are two potentially correct answers:

Neither Martha nor her sisters <u>are</u> going on vacation.
*or*
Neither her sisters nor Martha <u>is</u> going on vacation.

Note that only the first alternative above is presented by answer choice D.

## 2. Leader (✷)

**Choice A**
**Classification:** Subject-Verb Agreement
**Skill Rating:** Easy
**Snapshot:** This problem is included to show subject-verb agreement and to highlight the role of prepositional phrases in disguising the subject and verb.

The subject of a sentence determines the verb (i.e., singular subjects take singular verbs; plural subjects take plural verbs) and the subject of this sentence is "activities" (plural). The intervening phrase "of our current leader" is a prepositional phrase, and prepositional phrases can never contain the subject of a sentence. Mentally cut out this phrase. Since the subject is "activities," the verb is "have," not "has." Another distinction that needs to be drawn relates to the difference between "number" and "amount." The word "number" is used for countable items and "amount" for non-countable items. Therefore, we have no problem choosing choice A as the correct answer after applying only two rules—the first is a subject-verb agreement rule followed by the "number" versus "amount" diction distinction. Also, per choices B and D, the clause "has/have been significant in the increase" is not only awkward but also passive.

## 3. Marsupial (✷✷)

**Choice D**
**Classification:** Subject-Verb Agreement
**Skill Rating:** Medium
**Snapshot:** This follow-up problem is also included to highlight the role of prepositional phrases within subject-verb agreement.

The subject of the sentence is "pattern," which is singular, and a singular subject takes the singular verb "indicates." An additional way to eliminate choices A and B is through the redundant use of the words "might" and "possibility" which express the same idea; either "possibility" or "might" is required. Also, the use of "might" in choice D is better than "may" (choice E) because "might" more clearly indicates "possibility" than does "may" and "might." "Might" is also the correct choice when referring to past events. In choosing between choices D and E, the idiom "descendant of" is superior to the unidiomatic "descendant from." Finally, note that in choices B and C, "had," the auxiliary of "lived," should be deleted because the simple past tense is correct. The past perfect, which employs "had," is not required; the past perfect tense is used to refer to an action that precedes some other action also occurring in the past.

NOTE ⤚ This problem complements the previous one. The former problem contained a plural subject ("activities") and a single item in the prepositional phrase ("current leader"). This problem contains a singular subject ("pattern") and a plural item in the prepositional phrase ("changes").

## 4. Critics' Choice (✶✶)

**Choice A**
**Classification:** Subject-Verb Agreement
**Skill Rating:** Medium
**Snapshot:** This problem is included to highlight "there is/there are" constructions in which the subject of the sentence comes after, not before the verb.

The compound subject is plural—"well-developed plot <u>and</u> an excellent cast of characters"—and, therefore, requires the plural verb "are." Choices B, C, and E are out because of the incorrect verb "is." Choices C and D employ roundabout constructions that are inferior to "In this critically acclaimed film." Choice D also employs the passive construction "which has been critically acclaimed." Choice E rearranges the sentence, but still incorrectly employs the singular verb "is."

## 5. Recommendations (✲✲)

**Choice A**
**Classification:** Subject-Verb Agreement
**Skill Rating:** Medium
**Snapshot:** This problem is included to highlight gerund phrases, which, when acting as the subject of a sentence, are always singular.

The gerund phrase "Implementing the consultants' recommendations" is the subject of the sentence. As gerund phrases are always singular, the correct verb here is "is." In choice C, "expected result" requires the verb "is," whereas in choice D, "expected results" requires the verb "are." In choice E, the "it is" construction creates an unnecessarily weak opener and an awkward sentence style.

## 6. Valuation (✲✲✲)

**Choice E**
**Classification:** Pronoun Usage
**Skill Rating:** Difficult
**Snapshot:** This problem is included to highlight ambiguity arising from the use of personal pronouns, and seeks to clear up such ambiguity, not by replacing pronouns, but by rearranging the sentence itself. Part of the reason it garners a high difficulty rating is because the problem is long, and somewhat more difficult to read and analyze.

Choices A and B use the word "they" to refer to traditional businesses; this is illogical because traditional businesses are not growing, Internet companies are. Remember that a pronoun modifies the closest noun that precedes it. The structure in choice C makes it seem as if "financial formulas" are growing, and this, of course, is farcical.

Choices A and C use the awkward clause "do not apply to X in the same way as they do to Y." A more succinct rendition is found in choice E—"do not apply to X in the same way as to Y." In choices A, C, and E, the verb "apply" is more powerful and, therefore, superior to the noun form "applicability," which appears in choices B and D.

NOTE ∽ Beware of the high school "tall tale" that suggests you shouldn't begin a sentence with the word "because." If you learned this as a rule, forget it. According to the conventions of Standard Written English (SWE)—which, incidentally, this book abides by—the word "because" functions as a subordinating conjunction. Its use is effectively identical to that of "as" or "since," and we can think of these three words as substitutes. In short, there's actually no rule of grammar or style preventing us from beginning a sentence with the word "because."

## 7. Inland Taipan (✷✷)

**Choice D**
**Classification:** Pronoun Usage
**Skill Rating:** Medium
**Snapshot:** This problem is included to highlight the occasional need to add pronouns in order to remove ambiguity.

This form of ambiguous reference is subtle. The original sentence is missing "they," and without the pronoun, *they*, the word "treated" might refer to "poison" or "victims"; "treated" is only supposed to refer to "victims." In choice C, the pronoun "it" logically but incorrectly refers to "bite." Technically it is not the bite that needs to be treated but the actual victims. Choices A, C, and E erroneously employ the idiom "regarded to be" when the correct idiom is "regarded as."

## 8. Medicare (✶)

**Choice C**
**Classification:** Pronoun
**Skill Rating:** Easy
**Snapshot:** This problem is included to highlight the need to choose the correct pronoun—"it"—when referring to a collective singular noun or single inanimate object.

Choices A and B are incorrect because the pronoun "they" cannot refer to the House of Representatives. Not only is the House of Representatives a collective singular noun, but it is also an inanimate object; therefore, the proper pronoun choice is "it."

Choice D improperly employs the pronoun "it," which incorrectly refers to the House of Representatives rather than to Medicare legislation. Choice E may be the most passive of these sentences, in which the doer of the action, the House of Representatives, is now at the very back of the sentence.

In choice C, the pronoun "it" correctly refers to Medicare legislation. The subordinate clause "although the House of Representatives is considering Medicare legislation" is written in the active voice. The latter part of the sentence is written in the passive voice "without being significantly revised," and we have to be willing to accept this wording; it's the best of the remaining choices. For the record, two alternative wordings for the latter part of the sentence might include: "it is not expected to pass unless it is significantly revised" (active voice but employs two uses of the pronoun "it") and "it is not expected to pass without significant revision" (active voice but employs the nominalized "revision").

*NOTE* ✺ In general, the five most common signals of the passive voice include: "be," "was," "were," "been," and "being." In addition, the preposition "by" is also closely associated with the passive voice: e.g., "The ball was caught by the outfielder."

**9. Oceans (✲)**

**Choice C**
**Classification:** Pronoun Usage
**Skill Rating:** Easy
**Snapshot:** This problem is included to highlight an improper shift in voice, also known as a shift in point of view.

In choice A, the third-person singular pronoun "one" is improperly matched with the second-person pronoun "you." In choice B, the third-person singular "one" is improperly matched with the third-person plural "they." Pronouns must agree with their antecedents in number and person. The problem highlighted here is not that of agreement with respect to person, but number. In choice C, the third-person singular "one" is properly matched with third-person singular "he" or "she." Per choice D, the third-person singular noun "a person" is improperly matched with the second person "you." Per choice E, the third-person singular noun "a person" is improperly matched with the third-person plural pronoun "they." Pronouns must agree with their antecedents in number and person. The problem here is not agreement with respect to person, but number.

*NOTE* ↔ The following summarizes the do's and don'ts with respect to pronoun usage in terms of person and number:

1) "You" can only be matched with "you."

Only "you" goes with "you." After all, there is only one second-person pronoun—*you.*

2) "He," "she," "one," or "a person" can be matched with any one of "he," "she," "one," or "a person."

Any third-person singular pronoun (e.g., he, she, one) or third-person singular noun (e.g., a person) can be matched with another third-person pronoun or noun (notwithstanding that gender should match as well).

3) "You" cannot be matched with "he," "she," "one," or "a person."

The second person pronoun "you" does not match any third-person pronoun or noun.

4) "They" cannot be matched with "he," "she," "one," or "a person."

The third-person plural pronoun "they" does not match properly any third-person singular pronoun or noun. Note also that "a person" is a noun, not a pronoun.

## 10. Metal Detector (✲)

**Choice C**
**Classification:** Modification
**Skill Rating:** Easy
**Snapshot:** This problem is included to illustrate misplaced modifiers. In particular, an introductory modifying phrase (a phrase that begins the sentence) always modifies the first noun or pronoun that follows it (and which itself is in the subjective case). The general rule is that "modifying words or phrases should be kept close to the word(s) that they modify."

The only answer choice that is written in the active voice is choice C. The other four answer choices are written in the passive voice (the word "be" signals the passive voice. In choice A, coins and other valuables cannot *use* a metal detector; we must look for a person to act as the doer of the action. Choice E changes the meaning of the sentence, suggesting that the hobbyists bury the coins themselves. Whereas choices A and E are incorrect, choices B, C, and D are each grammatically correct. Choice C is the winner because, all things being equal, the active voice is deemed superior to the passive voice. This is a rule of style rather than grammar. Style is more or less effective, better or worse. Grammar is correct or incorrect, right or wrong.

*NOTE* ⤚ Modification may involve the replacement of individual qualifying words, such as *almost, only, just, even, hardly, nearly, not,* and *merely.* Ideally, these words should be placed immediately before or after the words they modify, lest they cause confusion.

In the memorable example below, consider how the placement of the word "only" changes the meaning of a single sentence.

Original        Life exists on earth.

Let's add the word "only" and vary its placement:

Example 1       Only life exists on earth.

                The meaning is that life is the sole occupier of earth. However, we know that there are things besides life that exist on earth, including inanimate objects like rocks.

Example 2       Life only exists on earth.

                The meaning is that life merely exists on earth and doesn't do anything else.

Example 3       Life exists only on earth.

                This is likely the intended meaning. The word "only" is appropriately placed in front of the word phrase it modifies—*on earth.*

Example 4       Life exists on only earth.

                The meaning here is the same as above but slightly more dramatic. The implication is that life's sole domain is earth, and we're proud of it.

Example 5       Life exists on earth <u>only</u>.

The meaning is also the same as example 3, but with a flair for the dramatic. The implication may be that life is found only on earth, and isn't that a shame.

## 11. Hungary (✶✶)

**Choice D**
**Classification:** Modification
**Skill Rating:** Medium
**Snapshot:** This problem is included to highlight a modification subtlety which necessitates the use of "account for" or "constitute."

Technically speaking, Hungarians don't *have* less than one percent of the world's population; they "account for" or "constitute" less than one percent of the world's population. This latter option is represented in choice D. The logic of choice E makes it incorrect. The transition words "in addition" are illogical because the sentence construction requires contrast, and the word "although" is consistent in this respect. For the record, another correct answer would have included: "Although accounting for less than one percent of the world's population, Hungarians have made disproportionately large contributions to the fields of modern math and applied sciences."

## 12. Natural Beauty (✶✶)

**Choice E**
**Classification:** Modification
**Skill Rating:** Medium
**Snapshot:** This problem is included to highlight another type of modification problem, known as "back sentence modification," because the phrase or clause set off by a comma occurs at the end of the sentence, not the beginning.

The final answer proves best—correct, logical, and succinct—in comparing *plastic surgery* to the act of *reconstructing a national park*. In short, the patient is being compared to a national park while the act of plastic surgery is being likened to the act of reconstructing a national park. The word "likening" functions as a participle; it introduces the participle phrase "likening it to reconstructing a national park." This phrase properly refers to "surgery," not "natural beauty."

In choices A, B, and C, the relative pronoun "which" refers, not to plastic surgery, but to the noun immediately preceding it, "(natural) beauty." As a result, natural beauty is compared to "reconstructing a national park" (choice A), to "a national park" (choice B), and to "reconstruction" (choice C). Choice D corrects this problem by eliminating the "which" construction and supplying the pronoun "it," thus referring clearly to "plastic surgery," but it illogically compares "plastic surgery" to "a national park." Moreover, the double use of "it" is awkward.

### 13. Cannelloni (✻)

**Choice D**
**Classification:** Parallelism
**Skill Rating:** Easy
**Snapshot:** This problem is included to highlight the use of parallelism as it relates to ellipsis (acceptable omission of words within a sentence).

To test choice D, simply complete each component idea, making sure each makes sense. "Cannelloni <u>has been</u> my favorite dish…Cannelloni always <u>will be</u> my favorite dish." Now check this against the original: "Cannelloni <u>was</u> my favorite dish (doesn't work)…Cannelloni always <u>will be</u> my favorite dish." Choice E suffers the same fate as choices A and B, erroneously omitting *has been*. Choices B and C are muddled; the word "was" illogically suggests that Cannelloni was once a favorite dish, but no longer is.

## 14. Massage (✶✶)

**Choice B**
**Classification:** Parallelism
**Skill Rating:** Medium
**Snapshot:** This problem is included to highlight the use of parallelism when using correlative conjunctions.

Correlative conjunctions include "either…or," "neither…nor," "not only…but (also)," and "both…and." The purpose of correlative conjunctions is to join ideas of equal weight. Therefore, things on both sides of each connector should be parallel in form and equal in weight.

The word pairing "both…as well as" is unidiomatic, so choice E can be eliminated. Here the correlative conjunction is "both…and," and the words that follow "both" and "and" must be parallel in structure. In choice B, the correct answer, the words "your body" follow "both" while the words "your well-being" follow "and"; this creates perfect parallelism. Choices C and D are not parallel. For the record, there are effectively two possibilities:

Massage creates a relaxing, therapeutic, and rejuvenating experience for <u>both</u> your body <u>and</u> your well-being.
*or*
Massage creates a relaxing, therapeutic, and rejuvenating experience <u>both</u> for your body <u>and</u> for your well-being.

Here's another example:

| | |
|---|---|
| Incorrect | Sheila <u>both</u> likes to act <u>and</u> to sing. |
| Correct | Sheila likes <u>both</u> to act <u>and</u> to sing. |
| *or* | |
| Correct | Sheila <u>both</u> likes to act <u>and</u> likes to sing. |

## 15. Europeans (✲✲✲)

**Choice A**
**Classification:** Parallelism
**Skill Rating:** Difficult
**Snapshot:** This problem is included to highlight the use of parallelism with regard to ellipsis, and to review semicolons, omission commas, sentence run-ons, and sentence fragments.

In choice A, the comma placed immediately after "France" and "Poland" is an *omission comma*—it takes the place of the missing words "is famous." See also *Appendix III – Punctuation Highlights*. Choice B provides an example of a run-on sentence. There must be an "and" preceding the word "Poland." As it stands, it is three sentences joined together by commas.

Choice C contains two sentence fragments: "France for its chefs and philosophers" and "Poland for its mathematicians and logicians." These phrases cannot stand on their own as complete sentences. Choice D improperly uses the pronoun "their," when what is called for is the pronoun "its." Moreover, we would need to have commas after both the words "France" and "Poland" in order to validate this choice; alternatively, we could omit commas after France and Poland. According to the rules of ellipsis, words can be omitted within a sentence if they're a readily understood in context.

Choice E changes the meaning of the original sentence (that's a no-no). There's little doubt that France and Poland have composers, musicians, chefs, philosophers, mathematicians, and logicians, but the focus is on what each country is specifically famous for.

In summary, there are four possible correct answers.

Correct          Italy is famous for its composers and musicians,
                 France is famous for its chefs and philosophers,

and Poland is famous for its mathematicians and logicians.

(The previous version repeats three times the words "is famous.")

Correct

Italy is famous for its composers and musicians, France, for its chefs and philosophers, and Poland, for its mathematicians and logicians.

(The above is the correct rendition per choice A. The comma after "France" and "Poland" is effectively taking the place of the words "is famous.")

Correct

Italy is famous for its composers and musicians, France for its chefs and philosophers, and Poland for its mathematicians and logicians.

(The above version is likely the most subtle. The rules of ellipsis allow us to omit words that are readily understood within the context of any sentence. The words "is famous" are readily understood. This version is almost identical to choice B, except that it correctly inserts the word "and," a coordinating conjunction, before Poland.)

Correct

Italy is famous for its composers and musicians; France, for its chefs and philosophers; Poland, for its mathematicians and logicians.

(The above version uses semicolons along with commas. Note that the final "and" before Poland is optional. Unlike choice D, this choice correctly inserts a comma after "France" and "Poland" and replaces the pronoun "their" with "its.")

## 16. Sweater (⋆)

**Choice E**
**Classification:** Comparisons
**Skill Rating:** Easy
**Snapshot:** This problem is included to highlight the handling of the comparative and superlative adjective forms.

The words "neither one" indicate that we are dealing with two sweaters. When comparing two things, we use the comparative form of the adjective, not the superlative. Thus, the correct choice is "better," not "best," and "smaller," not "smallest." "Better" and "smaller" (comparatives) are used when comparing exactly two things; "best" and "smallest" (superlatives) are used when comparing three or more things.

*NOTE* ↬ When two things are being compared, the *comparative* form of the adjective (or adverb) is used. The comparative is formed in one of two ways: (1) adding "er" to the adjective (for adjectives containing one syllable), or (2) placing "more" before the adjective (especially for adjectives with more than two syllables). Use one of the above methods, but never both: "Jeremy is wiser (or *more wise*) than we know," but never "Jeremy is more wiser than we know."

Some modifiers require internal changes in the words themselves. A few of these irregular comparisons are presented in the following chart:

| Positive | Comparative | Superlative |
|----------|-------------|-------------|
| good | better | best |
| well | better | best |
| bad | worse | worst |
| far | farther, further | farthest, furthest |
| late | later, latter | latest, last |
| little | less, lesser | least |
| many, much | more | most |

## 17. Sir Isaac Newton (✻)

**Choice E**
**Classification:** Comparisons
**Skill Rating:** Easy
**Snapshot:** This solution to this problem pivots on the use of the demonstrative pronoun "those."

The words "those" and "other" must show up in the correct answer. First, without the word "other," choices A, C, and D illogically compare Sir Isaac Newton to all scientists, living or dead, even though Sir Isaac Newton is one of those scientists. Second, without the word "those," choices A and B illogically compare "the accomplishments of Sir Isaac Newton" to "other scientists." Obviously, we must compare "the accomplishments of Sir Isaac Newton" to "the accomplishments of other scientists." In choices C, D, and E, the word "those" exists to substitute for the phrase "the accomplishments."

## 18. Soya (✻✻)

**Choice C**
**Classification:** Comparisons
**Skill Rating:** Medium
**Snapshot:** This problem highlights the use of the demonstrative pronoun "that."

Here, we must correctly compare "the protein in meat" to "the protein in soybeans." The demonstrative pronoun "that" is very important because it substitutes for the words "the protein." Choice C creates a sentence which effectively reads: "In addition to having more protein than meat does, the protein in soybeans is higher in quality than *the protein* in meat."

Choices A and B are out because the word "meat" must come after the opening phrase "in addition to having more protein than meat does." Choice D correctly employs "soybeans," but incorrectly uses "it" to make a comparison. The word "it" cannot stand for "the protein." Choice E incorrectly compares soybean protein to meat.

**19. Angel (✶✶)**

**Choice C**
**Classification:** Comparisons
**Skill Rating:** Medium
**Snapshot:** This problem is included to highlight proper comparisons involving "like" versus "as."

The basic difference between "like" and "as" is that "like" is used for phrases, and "as" is used for clauses. A phrase is a group of words that does not contain a verb; a clause is a group of words that does contain a verb. Choices D and E ungrammatically employ "as" in phrases, in addition to being awkwardly constructed.

There are three potentially correct versions:

1)  She sings <u>like an angel</u>.

    "Like an angel" is a phrase (there is no verb), so "like" is the correct choice.

2)  She sings <u>as an angel sings</u>.

    "As an angel sings" is a clause (contains the verb "sings"), so "as" is the correct choice.

3)  She sings <u>as an angel does</u>.

    "As an angel does" is a clause (contains the verb "does"), so "as" is the correct choice.

*NOTE* ◌ Advertising is an arena where violations in English grammar may be turned to advantage. The American cigarette company Winston once adopted the infectious advertising slogan: "Winston tastes good like a cigarette should." The ungrammatical and somehow proactive use of "like" instead of "as" created a minor sensation, helping to propel the brand to the top of the domestic cigarette market. A more recent advertising campaign by DHL in Asia also contains a grammatical violation: "No one knows Asia like we do." The correct version should read: "No one knows Asia as we do."

## 20. Perceptions (✳✳)

**Choice D**
**Classification:** Comparisons
**Skill Rating:** Medium
**Snapshot:** This problem is included to highlight the comparative idiom "as...do"/"as...does."

The problem pivots on the "like/as" distinction. The intended comparison is between the convergent thinking processes of right-brain individuals and the convergent thinking processes of left-brain individuals. We cannot compare the convergent thinking processes of right-brain individuals directly to left-brain individuals (per answer choices A and B). The verb "do" is needed in order to substitute for the ability of left-brain individuals to employ convergent thinking processes.

Choices C, D, and E use the correct connector, "as," which is used with clauses, while choices C and E use "like" or "unlike," which is used with phrases. Choices B and E use the singular "individual" rather than the plural "individuals." Either of the following would be better:

Correct        Unlike left-brained individuals, right-brained individuals often do not employ their attention or perceptions systematically, and they may not notice and remember the same level of detail <u>as</u> their left-brained counterparts <u>do</u>.

Correct        Right-brained individuals often do not employ their attention or perceptions systematically, and, unlike left-brained individuals, right-brain individuals may not notice and remember the same level of detail as their left-brained counterparts do.

## 21. Geography (✻✻)

**Choice A**
**Classification:** Comparisons
**Skill Rating:** Medium
**Snapshot:** This problem is included to highlight the correct use of the "more ... than" idiom, used in comparing two things.

Make an initial note that we should ideally be comparing American high school *students* with Canadian high school *students* (plural with plural) because the non-underlined part of the sentence contains the words "counterparts." Be suspicious of any of the answer choices which begin with "the American high school student." Verify also that in all cases verbs are correct. "Do" is a plural verb that matches the plural phrase "Canadian counterparts"; "does" is a singular verb that would be used to match the singular phrase "Canadian counterpart."

The last piece of the puzzle is to eliminate the non-standard comparative constructions, namely "more ... compared to" as well as "more ... compared with." The correct idiom is "more ... than" or "less ... than." This idiom appears on pages 154–155 and on page 219, as part of *200 Common Grammatical Idioms*. Thus, choices B, C, and E cannot be correct.

## 22. Assemblée Nationale (✶✶)

**Choice D**
**Classification:** Comparisons
**Skill Rating:** Medium
**Snapshot:** This problem is included to highlight the comparative idiom "Just as...so (too)." Note that the brackets indicate the optional use of the word "too."

In choices A and B, the use of "as" is incorrect. "As" functions as a subordinating conjunction, and this means that the reader expects a logical connection between the fact that Britain has a Parliament and France has the Assemblée Nationale. Try substituting the subordinating conjunction "because" in either choices A or B and the illogical relationship becomes more apparent. "Because Parliament is the legislative government body of Great Britain, the Assemblée Nationale is the legislative government body of France."

The "just as...so (too)" comparative idiom (choice D) can be used to express this type of meaning. "Just as something, so something else." Choice D provides a standard comparison: The Parliament of Great Britain is being compared to the Assemblée Nationale of France. In choice E, the comparison is awkward because we end up comparing the Government of Britain's Parliament with the Assemblée Nationale.

Choice C is awkward and "just like" is used with phrases, not clauses. Clearly we are dealing with a clause.

*NOTE* ✍ Savor this classic example:

| | |
|---|---|
| Correct | <u>Just as</u> birds have wings, <u>so too</u> do fish have fins. |
| Incorrect | As birds have wings, fish have fins. |
| Incorrect | As birds have wings, fish, therefore, have fins. |

Substituting "because" for "as" above, we can quickly see an illogical relationship. There is no logical connection between a bird's having wings and a fish's having fins. In other words, just because a bird has wings doesn't mean that a fish has to have fins.

## 23. Bear (✶✶✶)

**Choice C**
**Classification:** Comparisons
**Skill Rating:** Difficult
**Snapshot:** When making comparisons, the most basic rule is to make sure to compare like things. That is, compare apples with apples and oranges with oranges. This is particularly true when distinguishing between the characteristics of one thing to the characteristics of something else. In such cases, we must compare thing to thing, and characteristic to characteristic.

Here we want to compare "bears" with "bears" or "diets of bears" with "diets of bears." Choice A, the original, compares animals with diets by erroneously comparing the "Alaskan brown bear and most other members" of the bear family to the "diet" of the grizzly bear. Choice B is structurally sound ("those" is a demonstrative pronoun that takes the place of "the diets"), but unidiomatically refers to the "diets" of the grizzly bear. Idiomatic speech would require the use of "diet" to refer to a single bear species and "diets" to refer to more than one species of bear. Choice D uses the repetitious "Just like" (when "like" alone is sufficient), as well as the unidiomatic "diets." Choice E commits the original error in reverse. Now "diets" of the Alaskan brown bear and most other members of the bear family are being compared directly to "grizzly bears," instead of to the diet of "grizzly bears."

All of the following provide potentially correct answers:

1) Like the Alaskan brown bear and most other members of the bear family, <u>the grizzly bear</u> has a <u>diet</u> consisting of both meat and vegetation.

2) Like the Alaskan brown bear and most other members of the bear family, <u>grizzly bears</u> have a <u>diet</u> consisting of both meat and vegetation.

3) Like the <u>diets</u> of the Alaskan brown bear and most other members of the bear family, the <u>diet</u> of the grizzly bear consists of both meat and vegetation.

4) Like the <u>diets</u> of the Alaskan brown bear and most other members of the bear family, the <u>diet</u> of grizzly bears consists of both meat and vegetation.

**24. Smarts (✷✷✷)**

**Choice E**
**Classification:** Comparisons
**Skill Rating:** Difficult
**Snapshot:** This problem is included as an "oddball" to demonstrate that we do not always compare a singular item with a singular item or a plural item with a plural item (e.g., Miller Analogies Test versus IQ tests). In context, a situation may necessitate comparing a singular item with a plural item or vice versa. Here the "apples to apples, oranges to oranges" comparison involves comparing one type of test to another type of test while comparing the format of one such test to the formats of the other type of test.

Choices A and B erroneously compare "the Miller Analogies Test" with "the formats..." We want to compare "one exam" to "another exam," or "the format of one exam" to the "format of another exam," or "the formats of some exams" to the "formats of other exams." Although choice C looks like the winning answer, upon closer examination, we realize that a single format cannot itself vary considerably in terms of content and length. Choice D correctly employs "formats," but now the problem reverses itself: A single IQ test does not have "formats." Choice E correctly combines "IQ tests" in the plural with "formats" in the plural.

Here's a follow-up example in mirror image to the problem at hand:

Incorrect  Unlike Canadian football, which is played on a standardized field, American baseball is played on a <u>field</u> that varies considerably in shape and size.

Correct  Unlike Canadian football, which is played on a standardized field, American baseball is played on <u>fields</u> that vary considerably in shape and size.

## 25. Golden Years (✷)

**Choice E**
**Classification:** Verb Tenses
**Skill Rating:** Easy
**Snapshot:** This problem is included to illustrate the difference between the present perfect tense and the past perfect tense. The correct answer employs the present perfect tense.

Only choice E uses the correct tense (present perfect), observes parallelism, and is idiomatic. Because the sentence describes a situation that continues into the present, choices A and B are incorrect in using the past perfect tense ("had elected"). In choice E, the noun forms "to retire" (infinitive) and "face" are more closely parallel than are the noun forms "retirement" and "facing." Note also that the dual expressions "x rather than y" and "x instead of y" are, according to Standard Written English, equivalent.

## 26. Politics (✶✶)

**Choice D**
**Classification:** Verb Tenses
**Skill Rating:** Medium
**Snapshot:** This problem is included to highlight the past perfect tense and the precise use of the auxiliary "had" in forming this tense.

The original sentence contains two critical past tense verbs: "disapproved" and "conceded." It also contains the time word "later," as in "later conceded," which serves to further clarify the sequence of past events. This problem highlights an important characteristic of the past perfect tense, namely that "had" is used before the first of two past events. In this example, Senator John McCain "disapproved" before he "conceded." Thus, the auxiliary "had" must be placed before the first (not the second) of the two past events: "had disapproved...later conceded."

Choice A erroneously proposes a reversal in sequence ("disapproved...had later conceded"), while choice E doubles the use of "had" to create a verbal muddle ("had disapproved...had later conceded"). Both of these choices result in illogical alternatives. Choices B and C incorrectly employ the present perfect tense ("has") when the past perfect tense ("had") is what is called for.

*NOTE* ⤖ Another correct answer would have included the following:

"Although he disapproved of the political platform set forth by Senator Barack Obama during the 2008 U.S. presidential primaries, Senator John McCain later conceded..."

This option is also correct, although it doesn't use the past perfect tense. It instead uses two past tense verbs, namely "disapproved" and "conceded," and the temporal word "later." Because the sequence of tense is clear, the use of the auxiliary "had" is considered optional. Refer to the explanation given for Q75 in *Answers to the 100 Question Quiz* (see pages 166–171).

## 27. Trend (✶✶)

**Choice A**
**Classification:** Verb Tenses
**Skill Rating:** Medium
**Snapshot:** This problem is included to illustrate the difference between the past tense versus the past perfect tense and the present perfect tense. The correct answer uses the past tense.

Here, the past tense is all that is needed to refer clearly to the time frame in the past (1980–1990). In choice B, the present perfect tense "has continued" is inconsistent with the timing of an event that took place in the distant past. In choice C, the past perfect tense "had continued" is not required because we are not making a distinction between the sequence of two past tense events.

In choices D and E, the focus switches from a rise in the "percentage of people" to a rise in the "abrupt increase." This shift in meaning is unwarranted and incorrect. The pronouns "it" (choice D) and "which" (choice E) are ambiguous and could refer to either the "percentage of people" or an "abrupt increase." Moreover, choices D and E employ the passive constructions "there had been" and "there was"; these are considered weak sentence constructions and are best avoided.

## 28. Fire (✶✶)

**Choice B**
**Classification:** Verb Tenses
**Skill Rating:** Medium
**Snapshot:** This problem is included to highlight the difference between the past perfect tense and the past tense and/or the present perfect tense. The correct answer employs the past perfect tense. This problem also addresses the passive verb construction "had been"/"have been."

The solution to this problem is conceptually similar to that of the preceding problem. The auxiliary "had" must be used in conjunction with the first of two past tense events. In short, only choice B uses the verb tenses correctly to indicate that houses were built or heavily damaged prior to their being destroyed by fire. Choices A, C, and E illogically state that some houses were both destroyed <u>and</u> heavily damaged; "or" is needed to indicate that each of the houses suffered either one fate or the other. In using only the simple past tense (i.e., the verb tense "were"), choice A fails to indicate that the houses were built before the fires occurred. Choices D and E erroneously employ the present perfect tense, saying in effect that the houses "have been constructed" after they were destroyed or heavily damaged last year.

## 29. B-School (✶✶)

**Choice E**
**Classification:** Verb Tenses
**Skill Rating:** Medium
**Snapshot:** This problem is included to illustrate the difference between the future tense and the present perfect tense (both simple and progressive verb forms). The correct answer uses the future tense.

Since all answer choices contain the words "in the coming years," we definitely know we are dealing with the future, and choice E complements our search for a future tense. In choices A and B, the tense "have been becoming" (present perfect progressive tense in the passive voice) doesn't work. In choices C and D, the present perfect tense is also out. The present perfect tense is useful only for events that began in the past and touch the present. Here we need a tense that takes us into the future.

## 30. Summer in Europe (**)

**Choice C**
**Classification:** Verb Tenses
**Skill Rating:** Medium
**Snapshot:** This problem illustrates the correct use of the future perfect tense.

This problem requires the use of the future perfect tense. Choices A and B, by employing the construction "have reached," offer incorrect versions based on the present perfect tense. Choices D and E create erroneous alternatives by commingling past tense constructions with those in the future tense. Choice D presents an incorrect version which doubles up the present perfect tense "have reached" with the future perfect tense "will have backpacked."

Choice E mixes the past tense "reached" with the future perfect tense (in the progressive form). For the record, an equally correct answer would have been: "By the time we reached France, we had been backpacking for 12 weeks." This would represent the correct use of the past perfect tense. Of course, the original sentence clearly indicates that the travelers are looking into the future—they have not yet arrived in France.

The future perfect tense and the past perfect tense are very much opposite in terms of time frame but structurally similar. The following provides two additional ways to distinguish between these two tenses:

Past perfect tense: By the time something happened (second event), something else had already happened (first event).

Future perfect tense: By the time something happens (second event), something else will have already happened (first event).

# Appendixes

*If technique is of
no interest to a writer,
I doubt that the writer
is an artist.*

—Marianne Moore

# Appendix I – Summary of the 20 Writing Principles and the 40 Rules of Grammar

*Part I: Structure*

Principle 1        Write your conclusion and place it first.

Principle 2        Break your subject into two to four major parts and use a lead sentence.

Principle 3        Use transition words to signal the flow of your writing.

Principle 4        Use the six basic writing structures to put ideas in their proper order.

Principle 5        Finish discussing one topic before going on to discuss other topics.

*Part II: Style*

Principle 6        Use specific and concrete words to support what you say.

Principle 7        Add personal examples to make your writing more memorable.

Principle 8        Use simple words to express your ideas.

Principle 9        Make your writing clearer by dividing up long sentences.

Principle 10       Cut out redundancies, excessive qualification, and needless self-reference.

Principle 11       Favor active sentences, not passive sentences.

Principle 12       Avoid nominalizing your verbs and adjectives.

Principle 13    Express a series of items in consistent, parallel form.

Principle 14    Vary the length and beginnings of your sentences.

Principle 15    Write with a positive, personal tone.

Principle 16    Avoid using the masculine generic to refer to both genders.

*Part III: Readability*

Principle 17    Add more space around your writing to increase readability.

Principle 18    Make key words and phrases stand out.

Principle 19    Use headings and headlines to divide or summarize your writing.

Principle 20    Wait until your writing stands still before you call it finished.

*Part IV: Grammar*

Rule 1    "And" always creates a compound subject.

Rule 2    If two items joined by "and" are deemed to be a single unit, then the subject is considered singular, and a singular verb is required.

Rule 3    When the subject of a sentence consists of two items joined by "or," the subject may either singular or plural. If the two items joined by "or" are both singular, then the subject and verb are singular. If the two items joined by "or" are both plural, then the subject and verb are plural. If one of the two items joined by "or" is singular and the other plural, the verb matches the subject that comes after "or."

Rule 4    "Pseudo-compound subjects" do not make singular subjects plural.

Rule 5    Prepositional phrases (i.e., phrases introduced by a preposition) can never contain the subject of a sentence.

Rule 6    "There is/there are" and "here is/here are" constructions represent special situations where the verb comes before the subject, not after the subject.

Rule 7    When acting as subjects of a sentence, gerunds and infinitives are always singular and require singular verbs.

Rule 8    "-One," "-body," and "-thing" indefinite pronouns are always singular.

Rule 9    Certain indefinite pronouns—"both," "few," "many," and "several"—are always plural.

Rule 10   "Some" and "none" indefinite pronouns may be singular or plural.

Rule 11   In "either ... or" and "neither ... nor" constructions, the verb matches the subject which comes directly after the "or" or "nor."

Rule 12   Collective nouns denote a group of individuals (e.g., family, government, assembly, crew). If the collective noun refers to a group as a whole or the idea of oneness predominates, use a singular verb. If not, use a plural verb.

Rule 13      "The number" is a singular noun and takes a singular verb. "A number" is plural and takes a plural verb.

Rule 14      Percents or fractions, when followed by an "of phrase," can take a singular or plural verb. The key lies in determining whether the noun within the "of phrase" is singular or plural.

Rule 15      Measurements involving money (e.g., dollars, pounds), time (e.g., five years, the fifties), weight (e.g., pounds, kilograms), or volume (e.g., gallons, kilograms) are always singular and take singular verbs.

Rule 16      As a general guide, pronouns at or near the front of a sentence take their subjective forms; pronouns at or near the back of a sentence take their objective forms. The precise rule, however, is that pronouns take their subjective form when they are subjects of a verb; they take their objective form when they are objects of a verb.

Rule 17      Pronouns take their objective form when they are the direct objects of prepositions.

Rule 18      When forming comparisons using "than" or "as...as," supply any "missing words" (e.g., a verb in the examples below) in order to determine whether the subjective or objective form of the pronoun is correct.

Rule 19      Who vs. Whom. "Who" is the subjective form of the pronoun, and "whom" is the objective form of the pronoun. If "he," "she," or "they" can be substituted for a pronoun in context, the correct form is "who." If "him," "her," or "them" can be substituted for a pronoun in context, the correct form is "whom."

Rule 20    Do not use a reflexive pronoun (a pronoun ending in "-self") if an ordinary personal pronoun will suffice.

Rule 21    Pronouns must agree in number with their antecedents.

Rule 22    Pronouns should not be ambiguous in context. If a pronoun does not refer clearly to a specific noun, it results in a situation of "ambiguous pronoun reference."

Rule 23    "Pronoun shifts," also known as "shifts in point of view," involve the inconsistent matching of pronouns, either in terms of person or number. Within a single sentence (and perhaps within an entire paragraph or writing piece), first person should be matched with first person, second person matched with second person, and third person matched with third person. A common violation involves matching the third-person "one" or "a person" with the second-person "you." Another violation involves matching the third-person singular "he," "she," "one," or "a person" with the third-person plural "they."

Rule 24    A misplaced modifier refers to a word which, because of its placement within a sentence, no longer modifies what it originally was intended to modify.

Rule 25    A dangling modifier refers to a situation in which the thing being modified is absent from the sentence.

Rule 26       Occasionally, a modifier or modifying phrase may accidentally be placed where it could modify either of the two words or phrases. This situation results in a "squinting modifier." Because it is unclear which of two words or phrases are being modified, the writer should consider rewriting this sentence to clear up this ambiguity.

Rule 27       Whenever a sentence opens with a phrase or clause that is set off by a comma, check to make sure that the first word that follows the comma is properly being modified by the opening phrase or clause that precedes it.

Rule 28       Verbs should follow consistent form. Typically this means that all verbs should end in "-ed" or "-ing."

Rule 29       When prepositions are used before items in a series of three, there are two possibilities with regard to their use. Either a single preposition is used before the first item in a series (but not with the next two items) or prepositions are used before each item in the series.

Rule 30       Correlative conjunctions (e.g., "either … or," "neither … nor," "not only … but also," and "both … and") require that parallelism be maintained after each component part of the correlative.

Rule 31       Gerunds and infinitives should be presented in parallel form. Where possible, gerunds are matched with gerunds and infinitives are matched with infinitives.

Rule 32      At times we can acceptably omit words in a sentence and still retain clear meaning. To check for faulty parallelism (in this context also known as improper use of ellipsis), complete each sentence component and make sure that each part of the sentence can stand on its own.

Rule 33      The superlative ("-est") is used when comparing three or more persons or things; the comparative ("-er") is used when comparing exactly two persons or things.

Rule 34      Remember to compare the characteristics of one thing to the characteristics of another thing, not the characteristics of one thing directly to another thing.

Rule 35      Faulty or improper comparisons often leave out key words, particularly demonstrative pronouns such as "those" and "that," which are essential to meaning.

Rule 36      "Like" is used with phrases. "As" is used with clauses. A "phrase" is a group of related words that doesn't have both a subject and a verb. A "clause" is a group of related words that does have a subject and a verb. An easier way to remember the difference is to simply say, "A phrase is a group of words which doesn't have a verb; a clause is a group of words which does have a verb."

Rule 37      Consistent use of verb tenses generally requires that a single sentence be written solely in the present, past, or future tense.

Rule 38      The present perfect tense employs the verbs "has" or "have." The past perfect tense employs the auxiliary "had." The future perfect tense employs the verb form "will have."

Rule 39    The subjunctive mood uses the verb "were" instead of "was." The subjunctive mood is used to indicate a hypothetical situation—it may express a wish, doubt, or possibility. It is also used to indicate a contrary-to-fact situation.

Rule 40    Conditional statements are most commonly expressed in an "If...then" format, in which case an "if" clause is followed by a "results" clause. Confusion often arises as to whether to use "will" or "would." The choice between these verb forms depends on whether a given conditional statement involves the subjunctive. For situations involving the subjunctive, the appropriate verb form is "would." For situations not involving the subjunctive, the verb form is "will." A helpful hint is that "would" is often used in conjunction with "were"—the appearance of both these words within the same sentence is the telltale sign of the subjunctive.

## Appendix II — Editing Tune-up

Rarely does our educational system, or writing skills courses in the particular, include a segment on editing. Editing is to writing what an oil change and tune-up, washing, waxing, vacuuming, and chamoising are to automobile care. Not only does it influence how we feel about the final product, but it directly impacts how others perceive our work. Editing is its own skill set. It's an integral writing component that demands a separate, dedicated review.

## Part I – Editing Mechanics

**a vs. an.** Use "a" before a word in which the first letter of that word is a consonant or has the sound of a consonant. Note that some vowels have the sound of a consonant when pronounced as individual letters.

Example          a fortune (the letter "f" is a consonant)

Example          a B.S. degree (the letter "B" is a consonant)

Example          a u-turn (the letter "u" is pronounced "yoo")

Use "an" before a word in which the first letter of that word is a vowel or has the sound of a vowel. Note that some consonants sound like vowels when pronounced as individual letters.

Example          an ox (the letter "o" is a vowel)

Example          an M.S. degree (the letter "M" is pronounced "em")

Example          an honor (the letter "h" is silent so "an" is matched with the letter "o"—a vowel)

**Abbreviations (Latin).** The abbreviations "e.g." (meaning "for example") and "i.e." (meaning "that is") are constructed with two periods, one after each of the two letters, with a comma always following the second period. The forms "eg." or "ie." are not correct.

Below are three ways to present information using "for example."

Correct          A number of visually vibrant colors (e.g., orange, pink, and purple) are not colors that would normally be used to paint the walls of your home.

## LATIN ABBREVIATIONS AND THEIR MEANING

| Abbreviations | Meaning |
| --- | --- |
| c. | approximately |
| cf. | compare |
| e.g. | for example |
| etc. | and so forth |
| et al. | and others |
| ibid. | in the same place |
| i.e. | in other words; that is |
| op. cit. | in the work cited |
| sc. | which means |
| sic. | in these exact words |
| s.v. | under the word or entry |
| v. | consult |
| viz. | namely |

Correct    A number of visually vibrant colors, e.g., orange, pink, and purple, are not colors that would normally be used to paint the walls of your home.

Correct    A number of visually vibrant colors, for example, orange, pink, and purple, are not colors that would normally be used to paint the walls of your home.

Below are three ways to present information using "that is."

Correct        The world's two most populous continents
               (i.e., Asia and Africa) account for 75 percent of
               the world's population.

Correct        The world's two most populous continents,
               i.e., Asia and Africa, account for 75 percent of
               the world's population.

Correct        The world's two most populous continents,
               that is, Asia and Africa, account for 75 percent
               of the world's population.

The Latin abbreviations listed in the chart on the previous page
should be used with caution. Their use depends on whether the
intended audience is likely to be familiar with their meaning.
This compilation is not so much an endorsement for their use as
it is a convenient list in case readers find them in various works.

*NOTE* ✍ The abbreviation "etc." stands for "et cetera" and translates as "and so forth." Never write "and etc." because "and" is
redundant and otherwise reads "and and so forth." See *Appendix
IV – American English vs. British English* for additional coverage
of abbreviations.

**Apostrophes for omitted letters.** When apostrophes are used to
represent omitted letters, they are always "nines" not "sixes."
This means they curl backwards not forwards.

Example        rock 'n' roll (not rock 'n' roll)

Example        jivin' (not jivin')

Example        'tis (not 'tis)

**Bulleted lists.** Displaying information vertically is often done with bulleted lists or numbered lists. The following provides a succinct summary on how to punctuate bulleted (or numbered) information. There are five basic scenarios. The topic chosen is one dear to us all—books!

*Scenario 1A*

Four words that describe why books are cool:

- durability
- accessibility
- portability
- affordability

Treatment: Here, a complete sentence introduces a bulleted list and the original sentence is appropriately followed by a colon. No periods follow any line of bulleted information because none is a complete sentence. Capitalization of these words is optional; however, for the sake of consistency, each of these words should begin with a capital letter or each word should be placed in lowercase (no capital letters).

*Scenario 1B*

Four reasons why printed books are great:

1. Durability
2. Accessibility
3. Portability
4. Affordability

Treatment: Numbered lists are punctuated identically to bulleted lists. The one exception is that the first word that follows each number must be capitalized. Note that numbered lists are not recommended unless there is a reason for their use, including the need to impose order or hierarchy.

*Scenario 2*

Why will printed books never become obsolete?

- They're durable.
- They're accessible.
- They're portable.
- They're affordable.

Treatment: The complete sentence that introduces the list above is appropriately followed, in context, by a question mark, not a colon. Since each line of bulleted information is a complete sentence, each begins with a capital letter and ends with a period.

*Scenario 3*

People love printed books because they're

- durable
- accessible
- portable
- affordable

Treatment: No colon is used after the word "they're" because it does not introduce a complete sentence. No periods follow any of the bulleted information because none is a complete sentence. Capitalization of the first word following each bullet is optional.

*Scenario 4*

Printed books are here to stay because

- They're highly durable.
- They're easily accessible.
- They're wonderfully portable.
- They're eminently affordable.

Treatment: The bulleted information above is not introduced by a complete sentence and no colon is used after the word "because." The beginning word of each bullet point is capitalized and a period ends each complete sentence.

*Scenario 5*

People love printed books because they're

- highly durable;
- easily accessible;
- wonderfully portable;
- eminently affordable.

Treatment: Because the bulleted information reads as a single sentence, it is possible to use a semicolon to separate bulleted information and use a period on the last line. However, if bulleted information is short, as in the examples above, it may be better to enumerate the list in run-in text rather than displaying information vertically. For example: People love printed books because they're (1) highly durable, (2) easily accessible, (3) wonderfully portable, and (4) eminently affordable.

A note on using periods: Periods are often used with bulleted information, as is the case with résumés or slide presentations. Inconsistency arises when periods are used arbitrarily, appearing at the end of one bulleted point but not another. Again, the "hard" rule is to put a period at the end of any bulleted information that forms a complete sentence and omit any period at the end of any bulleted information that does not form a complete sentence. However, an arguably more practical rule of thumb with respect to résumés or slide presentations would be to omit a period after any short bulleted information (say six or fewer words) and include periods after any bulleted information that extends more than a line in length (regardless of whether or not it forms a complete sentence). The rationale for erring on the side of including periods is that a period helps create closure for the eye, thereby enhancing readability.

**Colon.** A colon (a punctuation mark that consists of two vertical dots) is commonly used to introduce a list or series of items and is often used after, or immediately after, the words "follow(s)," "following," "include(s)," or "including." A colon is not used after the words *namely, for example, for instance,* or *such as.* When introducing a list or series of items, a colon is also not used after forms of the verb "to be" (i.e., *is, are, am, was, were, have been, had been, being*) or after "short" prepositions (e.g., *at, by, in, of, on, to, up, for, off, out, with*).

Incorrect        We sampled several popular cheeses, namely:
                 Gruyere, Brie, Camembert, Roquefort, and
                 Stilton.

                 (Remove the colon placed after the word "namely.")

Incorrect        My favorite video game publishers are:
                 Nintendo, Activision, and Ubisoft.

                 (Remove the colon placed after the verb "are.")

Incorrect        Graphic designers should be proficient at:
                 Photoshop, Illustrator, InDesign, and Adobe
                 Acrobat.

                 (Remove the colon placed after the preposition
                 "at.")

However, if what follows a colon is <u>not</u> a list or series of items, the writer is free to use the colon after any word that he or she deems fit.

Correct          The point is: People who live in glass houses
                 shouldn't throw stones.

                 (A colon follows the verb "is.")

Correct          Warren Buffett went on: "Only four things
                 really count when making an investment—a

> business you understand, favorable long-term
> economics, able and trustworthy management,
> and a sensible price tag. That's investment.
> Everything else is speculation."

(A colon follows the preposition "on.")

**Compound adjectives.** Compound adjectives (also called compound modifiers) occur when two (or more) words act as a unit to modify a single noun. With reference to the chart on the following page, use a hyphen to join the compound adjective when it comes before the noun it modifies, but not when it comes after the noun.

Note that in situations where compound adjectives are formed using multiple words and/or words that are already hyphenated, it is common practice to use an en dash (–) to separate them. See entry under *Dashes*.

Example          Los Angeles–Buenos Aires

Example          quasi-public–quasi-private health care bill

Sometimes compound adjectives consist of a string of "manufactured" words.

Example          a fly-by-the-seat-of-your-pants entrepreneur

Example          a tell-it-like-it-is kind of spokesperson

There are four potentially confusing situations where compound adjectives are either not formed or not hyphenated. The first occurs where a noun is being modified by an adjective and an adjective is being modified by an adverb.

Example          very big poster

In the previous example, "big" functions as an adjective describing the noun "poster," and "very" functions as an adverb describing the adjective "big."

## COMPOUND ADJECTIVES

| Compound adjectives (hyphenated) | Non-compound adjectives (not hyphenated) |
| --- | --- |
| Experience teaches a person to use a step-by-step approach when solving problems.<br><br>"Step by step" comes before the noun "approach," so it is hyphenated. | Experience teaches a person to approach solving problems step by step.<br><br>"Step by step" comes after the noun "approach," so it is not hyphenated. |
| Send a follow-up e-mail. | Send an e-mail to follow up. |
| Write an in-depth report. | The report discussed the topic in depth. |
| An informative and up-to-date newsletter. | A newsletter that is informative and up to date. |
| A well-known person. | A person who is well known. |
| A well-intentioned act. | An act that is well intentioned. |
| Five brand-new bikes. | Five bikes that are brand new. |
| The ten-year-old girl. | The girl who is ten years old. |
| A thirty-five-year-old CEO. | A CEO who is thirty-five years old. |

The second situation occurs when adjectives describe a compound noun: that is, two words that function as a single noun.

Example          cold roast beef

Here the word "cold" functions as an adjective to describe the compound noun "roast beef." We would not write "cold-roast beef" because "cold-roast" does not jointly modify "beef."

Example          little used book

Here the word "little" functions as an adjective to describe the compound noun "used book." The meaning here is that the book is not new and also little. However, it would also be correct to write "little-used book" if our intended meaning was that the book was not often referred to.

A third situation occurs when a compound noun describes another noun.

Example          high school student

Example          cost accounting issues

"High school" is considered a compound noun that describes "student." Compound nouns are not hyphenated. "Cost accounting," which describes "issues," is also a non-hyphenated compound noun.

A fourth situation occurs when compounds are formed with adverbs ending in "ly." Adverbs ending in "ly" are not hyphenated, even when functioning as compound modifiers.

Example          a highly motivated employee

Example          a newly published magazine

Example          a publicly traded company

Example          a frequently made error

*NOTE* ✍ "Family-owned" and "family-run" are hyphenated (when functioning as compound adjectives) because "family," although ending in "ly," is not an adverb.

**Dashes.** Note first the difference between a hyphen and a dash. A dash is longer than a hyphen (-) and should not be used when what is needed is a dash. There are two types of dashes. The first is called "em dash" ("—"), which is the longer of the two dashes. The second is called "en dash" ("–"), which is the shorter of the two dashes. The en dash (–) is most popular in everyday writing, while the em dash (—) is the standard convention for formal published documents. Incidentally, the en dash is so-called because it is the width of the capital letter "N"; the em dash is so-called because it is the width of the capital letter "M." These two types of dashes can be found in Microsoft Word® under the pull-down menu Insert, Symbols, Special Characters.

Three common conventions arise relating to the use of the dash: (1) an en dash (" – ") with spaces on both sides of the dash, (2) an em dash ("—") with no spaces on either side of the dash, and (3) an em dash (" — ") with spaces on both sides of the dash. The first two conventions are the most popular for written (non-published) documents. The third option is popular on websites.

Example     To search for wealth or wisdom – that's a classic dilemma.

(Spaces on both sides of the en dash.)

Example     To search for wealth or wisdom—that's a classic dilemma.

(No space on either side of the em dash.)

Example     To search for wealth or wisdom — that's a classic dilemma.

(Space on both sides of the em dash.)

**Hyphen.** Use a hyphen with compound numbers between twenty-one through ninety-nine and with fractions.

Example          Sixty-five students constitute a majority.

Example          A two-thirds vote is necessary to pass.

In general, use a hyphen to separate component parts of a word in order to avoid confusion with other words especially in the case of a double vowel.

Example          Our goal must be to re-establish dialogue, then
                 to re-evaluate our mission.

Example          Samantha's hobby business is turning shell-
                 like ornaments into jewelry.

Use a hyphen to separate a series of words having a common base that is not repeated.

Example          small- to medium-sized companies

                 (This of course is the shortened version of
                 "small-sized to medium-sized companies.")

Example          short-, mid-, and long-term goals

                 (This is the shortened version of "short-term,
                 mid-term, and long-term goals.")

In general, use hyphens with the prefixes *ex-* and *self-* and in forming compound words with *vice-* and *elect-*.

Example          Our current vice-chancellor, an ex-commander,
                 is a self-made man.

*NOTE* ✍ "Vice president" (American English) is not hyphenated, but "vice-presidential duties" is.

**Numbers.** The numbers one through one hundred, as well as any number beginning a sentence, are spelled out. Numbers above 100 are written as numerals (e.g., 101).

| | |
|---|---|
| Original | Our professor has lived in 3 countries and speaks 4 languages. |
| Correct | Our professor has lived in <u>three</u> countries and speaks <u>four</u> languages. |

**Plural nouns.** Watch for situations involving the personal pronouns "they" and "our" that require that they be matched with plural nouns, not singular nouns. This occurs when a noun is not identical for all members of a group. "Our dream" and "our dreams" pose different meanings.

| | |
|---|---|
| Incorrect | Candidates should bring their <u>résumé</u> to their job <u>interview</u>. |
| Correct | Candidates should bring their <u>résumés</u> to their job <u>interviews</u>. |
| Incorrect | When it comes to computers, some people don't have a technical bone in their <u>body</u>. |
| Correct | When it comes to computers, some people don't have a technical bone in their <u>bodies</u>. |

**Possessives.** Confusion can arise regarding how to create possessives with respect to nouns. There are four basic situations. These involve (1) creating possessives with respect to single nouns not ending in "s"; (2) creating possessives with respect to single nouns ending in "s"; (3) creating possessives for plural nouns not ending in "s"; and (4) creating possessives for plurals ending in "s."

For <u>single nouns</u> not ending in the letter "s," we simply add an apostrophe and the letter "s" (i.e., 's).

Example          Jeff's bike

Example          The child's baseball glove

For <u>single nouns</u> ending in the letter "s," we have a choice of either adding an apostrophe and the letter "s" (i.e., 's) or simply an apostrophe.

Example          Professor Russ's lecture

Example          Professor Russ' lecture

For <u>plural nouns</u> not ending in the letter "s," we simply add an apostrophe and the letter "s" (i.e., 's).

Example          men's shoes

Example          children's department

For <u>plural nouns</u> ending in the letter "s," we simply add an apostrophe. Note that most plural nouns do end in the letter "s."

Example          ladies' hats

Example          The boys' baseball bats

In this latter example, "boys' baseball bats" indicates that a number of boys have a number of (different) baseball bats. If we were to write "boys' baseball bat," it would indicate that a number of boys all own or share the same baseball bat. If we wrote "the boy's baseball bat," only one boy would own the baseball bat. In writing "the boy's baseball bats," we state that one boy possesses several baseball bats.

**Print out to edit.** Where possible, do not perform final edits on screen. Print documents out and edit from a hard copy.

**Quotations.** The following four patterns are most commonly encountered when dealing with quotations.

Example       My grandmother said, "An old picture is like a
              precious coin."

Example       "An old picture is like a precious coin," my
              grandmother said.

              (A comma is generally used to separate the
              quote from regular text.)

Example       "An old picture," my grandmother said, "is like
              a precious coin."

              (Above is what is known as an interrupted or
              split quote. The lower case "i" in the word "is"
              indicates that the quote is still continuing.)

Example       "They're like precious coins," my grandmother
              said. "Cherish all your old pictures."

              (Above are two complete but separate quotes.
              Note the word "cherish" is capitalized because
              it begins a new quote.)

With respect to American English, there is a punctuation "tall tale" that suggests using double quotation marks when quoting an entire sentence, but using single quotation marks for individual words and phrases. There is, however, no authoritative support for this practice. The only possible use for single quotation marks in American English is for a quote within a quote. For more on the use of double or single quotation marks, see *Appendix IV – American English vs. British English*.

**Quotation marks.** There are two different styles of quotation marks: straight quotes and curly quotes. Straight quotes are also known as computer quotes or typewriter quotes. Curly quotes are commonly referred to as smart quotes or typographer's quotes.

For the purpose of <u>written</u> (printed) documents, we want to make sure we always use curly quotes and avoid straight quotes:

| Correct | I didn't say, "I'm not happy." (curly quotes) |
|---|---|

| Incorrect | I didn't say, "I'm not happy." (straight quotes) |
|---|---|

We want to avoid commingling straight quotes with curly quotes in any given document. Remember, we use "sixes" (" or ') and "nines" (' or ") for printed documents, but not straight quotes. Straight quotes find their way into a word processing document as text is copied and pasted from e-mail attachments. A good tip for getting rid of straight quotes in any word document is to use the Find/Replace feature, which is included with any word processing application.

**Slashes.** A slash (also known as a virgule) is commonly used to separate alternatives. No space should be used on either side of the slash; the slash remains "sandwiched between letters."

| Incorrect | At a minimum, a résumé or CV should contain a person's job responsibilities <u>and / or</u> job accomplishments. |
|---|---|

| Correct | At a minimum, a résumé or CV should contain a person's job responsibilities <u>and/or</u> job accomplishments. |
|---|---|

**Standard vs. nonstandard words and phrases.** Because language changes over time, complete agreement never exists as to what grammatical words and phrases are considered standard. From one grammar handbook to another and from one dictionary to another, slight variations arise. These differences are due in large part to the differences between colloquial and formal written language. For example, in colloquial written English, the words "all right" and "alright" as well as "different from" and "different than" are used interchangeably. Lexicographers continue to have difficulty deciding whether to prescribe language or describe it. Should they prescribe and dictate what are the correct forms of language, or should they describe and record language as it is used by a majority of people? The chart that follows provides common misusages to watch for.

## STANDARD VS. NONSTANDARD USAGES

| Standard | Nonstandard |
|---|---|
| After all, a lot, all right | Afterall, alot, alright |
| Anywhere, everywhere, nowhere | Anywheres, everywheres, nowheres |
| Because, since, as (when these words are used as a conjunction meaning "for the reason that") | Being as/being that |
| Could have/would have/ should have/might have/ may have | Could of/would of/should of/might of/may of |
| Every time (always written as two words) | Everytime |
| Himself, themselves | Hisself, theirselves |
| In comparison to | In comparison with |
| In contrast to | In contrast with |
| In regard to, with regard to | In regards to, with regards to, in regards of |
| Regardless | Irregardless |
| Supposed to/used to | Suppose to/use to |
| The reason is that | The reason is because |

**Titles and capitalization.** With respect to books, magazines, songs, etc., confusion often exists as to when titles are italicized and when they are placed in quotation marks. Note that underlining is no longer used to identify titles (gone are the days of the typewriter). The general rule is that longer works or full works are placed in italics. Partial works or short works are placed in quotation marks, and are not italicized. This means that the titles of books, magazines, newspapers, movies, TV programs, radio programs, plays, and names of albums are italicized. However, the titles of articles, essays, short stories, poems, chapters in a book, episodes in a TV series, and songs are placed in quotation marks.

Three rules are always observed with regard to the capitalization of titles—always capitalize the first and last words of a title and never use a period after the last word. Beyond this, the rules for capitalization of titles are somewhat arbitrary. The broad rule is to capitalize all "important" words and not to capitalize small, "unimportant" words. "Important" words include all nouns, pronouns, verbs, adjectives, and adverbs. Exceptions may include the verbs "is," "am," and "are" and the word "as," regardless of what part of speech it represents. "Unimportant" words—prepositions, conjunctions, and interjections—may or may not be capitalized. Two-letter prepositions (e.g., *at, by, in, of, on, to, up*) are seldom capitalized and the articles (i.e., *a, an, the*) are virtually never capitalized (unless, of course, they're the first word of a title). The coordinating conjunctions *and, but, or, nor,* and *for* are seldom capitalized; the coordinating conjunctions *yet* and *so* are almost always capitalized.

*NOTE* ✒ Some confusion may arise with regard to the words "capitalization" and "full caps." Capitalization denotes placing only the first letter of a word in caps (e.g., Great). Full caps refers to placing every letter of a word in caps. (e.g., GREAT).

## Part II — Editing for Style and Layout

**Brevity.** As a general rule, less is more. Consider options that express the same ideas in fewer words without changing the meaning of a sentence.

| | |
|---|---|
| Less effective | A movie director's <u>skill</u>, <u>training</u>, and <u>technical ability</u> cannot make up for a poor script. |
| More effective | A movie director's <u>skill</u> cannot make up for a poor script. |

Often you can cut "of" or "of the."

| | |
|---|---|
| Original | employees of the company |
| Better | company employees |

Don't use "due to the fact that" or "owing to the fact that." Use "because" or "since."

| | |
|---|---|
| Original | <u>Owing to the fact that</u> questionnaires are incomplete, it is difficult to draw definitive conclusions. |
| Better | <u>Because</u> questionnaires are incomplete, it is difficult to draw definitive conclusions. |
| Original | We want to hire the second candidate <u>due to the fact that</u> he is humorous and has many good ideas. |
| Better | We want to hire the second candidate <u>since</u> he is humorous and has many good ideas. |

**Bullets vs. hyphens or asterisks.** Bullets are most commonly used with résumés and flyers, but they are also welcomed companions in nonfiction, especially when used with lists or tables. It is not considered good practice in formal writing to use hyphens (-) or asterisks (*) in place of bullets. Standard protocol requires use of round bullets, square bullets, or perhaps webdings, wingdings, or dingbats—these "dings" represent ornamental bullets or tiny graphical characters.

Examples include: ● , • , ○ , ■ , ▪ , ◆ , ♦ , ◇ , ▶ , ▼ , ❑ , ⇨ , ➢

**Nominalizations.** A guiding rule of style is that we should prefer verbs (and adjectives) to nouns. Verbs are considered more powerful than nouns. In other words, a general rule in grammar is that we shouldn't change verbs (or adjectives) into nouns. The technical name for this no-no is "nominalization"; we shouldn't nominalize.

Avoid changing verbs into nouns:

| | |
|---|---|
| More effective | reduce costs |
| Less effective | reduction of costs |
| | |
| More effective | develop a five-year plan |
| Less effective | development of a five-year plan |
| | |
| More effective | rely on the data |
| Less effective | reliability of the data |

In the above three examples, the more effective versions represent verbs, not nouns. So "reduction of costs" is best written "reduce costs," "development of a five-year plan" is best written "develop a five-year plan," and "reliability of the data" is best written "rely on the data."

Avoid changing adjectives into nouns:

| | |
|---|---|
| More effective | precise instruments |
| Less effective | precision of the instruments |
| | |
| More effective | creative individuals |
| Less effective | creativity of individuals |
| | |
| More effective | reasonable working hours |
| Less effective | reasonableness of the working hours |

In the latter three examples above, the more effective versions represent adjectives, not nouns. So "precision of instruments" is best written "precise instruments," "creativity of individuals" is best written "creative individuals," and "reasonableness of the working hours" is best written "reasonable working hours."

**Page numbering.** A time-honored convention in publishing is that odd-numbered pages are "right-hand" pages and all pages are counted, whether or not a page number is printed on a page. In the case of a nonfiction book, this means that page 1 is typically the title page (no page number is printed), page 2 is the copyright page (no page is number printed), page 3 is the table of contents (the page number may or may not be printed), page 5 is the introduction (the page number is printed), and so forth.

In the case of a business report, page 1 is the title page (no page number is printed), page 3 is often the executive summary (the page number may or may not be printed), page 5 is the table of contents (the page number may or may not be printed), page 7 is the introduction (the page number is printed), and so forth.

Obviously the exact types of information included in a book, report, or academic research paper will vary, but three page-formatting conventions will always be adhered to. First, odd-numbered pages will always be right-hand or front pages and even-numbered pages will always be left-hand or backside pages. Second, all pages will count toward the total number of pages. Third, all new sections begin as odd-numbered, right-hand pages (with few exceptions). This means that if one section ends on an odd-numbered page, then the next page will be "skipped" so that the next section can begin on an odd-numbered page. The page that was skipped (an even numbered, left-hand page) remains blank, and although no page number is printed on it, it tallies in the page count as would an actual, fully printed page. Following these three conventions helps ensure that long documents look professionally laid out.

**Paragraph styles.** Two basic formats may be followed when laying out a written document: "block-paragraph" format and "indented-paragraph" format. The block-paragraph format typifies the layout of the modern business letter. Each paragraph is followed by a single line space (one blank line). Paragraphs are blocked, meaning that every line aligns with the left-hand margin with no indentation. Often, paragraphs are fully justified, which means there are no "ragged edges" on the right-hand side of any paragraph.

The indented-paragraph format is the layout followed in a novel. The first line of each paragraph is indented and there is no line space used between paragraphs within a given chapter. Note, however, that the first line of opening paragraphs, those that begin a new chapter, are not indented (they are left justified).

Whereas the indented-paragraph format (with indented paragraphs) usually has the effect of making writing look more personable—more like a story—the block-paragraph format (typically with fully justified paragraphs) lends a more formal appearance.

**Passive voice vs. active voice.** As a general rule of style, write in the active voice, not in the passive voice (all things being equal).

| | |
|---|---|
| Less effective | Sally <u>was</u> loved by Harry. |
| More effective | Harry loved Sally. |
| Less effective | In pre-modern times, medical surgery <u>was</u> often performed by inexperienced and ill-equipped practitioners. |
| More effective | In pre-modern times, inexperienced and ill-equipped practitioners often performed medical surgery. |

In a normal subject-verb-object sentence, the doer of the action appears at the front of the sentence while the receiver of the action appears at the back of the sentence. Passive sentences are less direct because they reverse the normal subject-verb-object sentence order; the receiver of the action becomes the subject of the sentence and the doer of the action becomes the object of the sentence. Passive sentences may also fail to mention the doer of the action.

| | |
|---|---|
| Less effective | Errors <u>were</u> found in the report. |
| More effective | The report contained errors. |
| *or* | The <u>reviewer</u> found errors in the report. |
| Less effective | Red Cross volunteers should <u>be</u> generously praised for their efforts. |
| More effective | <u>Citizens</u> should generously praise Red Cross volunteers for their efforts. |
| *or* | <u>We</u> should generously praise Red Cross volunteers for their efforts. |

How can we recognize a passive sentence? Here's a quick list of six words that signal a passive sentence: *be, by, was, were, been,* and *being.* For the record, "by" is a preposition, not a verb form, but it frequently appears in sentences that are passive.

**Qualifiers.** Whenever possible, clean out qualifiers, including: *a bit, a little, fairly, highly, just, kind of, most, mostly, pretty, quite, rather, really, slightly, so, still, somewhat, sort of, very,* and *truly.*

| | |
|---|---|
| Original | Our salespeople are <u>just</u> not authorized to give discounts. |
| Better | Our salespeople are not authorized to give discounts. |
| Original | That's <u>quite</u> a big improvement. |
| Better | That's a big improvement. |

Original          Working in Reykjavik was a <u>most</u> unique
                  experience.

Better            Working in Reykjavik was a unique experience.

*NOTE* ❧ Unique means "one of a kind." Something cannot be somewhat unique, rather unique, quite unique, very unique, or most unique, but it can be rare, odd, or unusual.

**Redundancies.** Delete redundancies. Examples: Instead of writing "continued on," write "continued." Rather than writing "join together," write "join." Instead of writing "serious disaster," write "disaster." Rather than writing "tall skyscrapers," write "skyscrapers." Instead of writing "past history," write "history."

**Sentence openers.** Can we begin sentences with the conjunctions "and" or "but"? There is a grammar folk tale that says we shouldn't begin sentences with either of these two words, but, in fact, it is both common and accepted practice in standard written English to do so. Most writers and journalists have embraced the additional variety gained from opening sentences in this manner. It is also acceptable to begin sentences with "because." In the same way that the words "as" and "since" are often used to begin sentences, the word "because," when likewise functioning as a subordinating conjunction, may also be used to begin sentences.

**Space: Break up long paragraphs.** Avoid long paragraphs in succession. Break them up whenever possible. This applies to e-mails as well. Often it is best to begin an e-mail with a one- or two-sentence opener before expounding on details in subsequent paragraphs.

**Space: Never two spaces after periods.** Avoid placing two spaces after a period (ending a sentence). Use one space. Computers automatically "build in" proper spacing. Leaving two spaces is a carryover from the days of the typewriter.

**Spacing within tables.** The most common editing error when presenting tables involves adequate spacing. A practitioner's rule is to leave, within any table cell, approximately one line space above the beginning line of type and below the ending line of type. In other words, don't let the lines of the table suffocate the type. Another important thing, if using bullet points within tables, is to make sure hanging indents line up. That is, text that flows from line to another should line up below its respective bullet point.

**Weak openers.** Limit the frequent use of sentences which begin with *it is, there is, there are,* and *there were.* These constructions create weak openers. A sound practice is to never begin the first sentence of a paragraph (i.e., the opening sentence) with this type of construction.

| | |
|---|---|
| Original | <u>It is</u> obvious that dogs make better pets than hamsters. |
| Better | Dogs make better pets than hamsters. |
| Original | <u>There is</u> an excellent chance that a better diet will make you feel better. |
| Better | A better diet will make you feel better. |

## Appendix III – Punctuation Highlights

In spoken English, we can convey our meaning through voice and body language: waving hands, rolling eyes, raising eyebrows, stress, rhythm, intonations, pauses, and even repeated sentences. In written language, we do not have such an arsenal of props; this is the unenviable job of punctuation. Mastery of punctuation, along with spelling, requires further review, and is not the focus of this book. But two key areas—commas and semicolons—are addressed because they represent areas where some of the most common punctuation errors occur.

## The Six Classic Uses of Commas

It is said that ninety percent of writers can use the comma correctly seventy-five percent of the time, but only one percent of writers can use the comma correctly ninety-nine percent of the time. The comma is often used, but often used incorrectly. The well-known advice that a comma be used whenever there is a pause is terribly misleading. Arguably the best way to master the comma is to think of every comma as fitting into one of six categories: listing comma, joining comma, bracketing comma, contrasting comma, omission comma, or confusion comma.

### Listing Comma

A listing comma separates items in a series. If more than two items are listed in a series, they should be separated by commas. The final comma in the series, the one that precedes the word *and,* is required. See *Appendix IV – American English vs. British English* for further discussion about the use of a comma before a final "and" or "or."

Correct   A tostada is usually topped with a variety of ingredients, such as shredded meat or chicken, refried beans, lettuce, tomatoes, and cheese.

Do not place commas before the first element of a series or after the last element.

Incorrect   The classic investment portfolio consists, of stocks, bonds, and short-term deposits.

      (Remove the comma placed after the word "consists.")

Correct   The classic investment portfolio consists of stocks, bonds, and short-term deposits.

| Incorrect | Conversation, champagne, and door prizes, were the highlights of our office party. |
|---|---|
| | (Remove the comma placed after the word "prizes.") |
| Correct | Conversation, champagne, and door prizes were the highlights of our office party. |

## Bracketing Comma

There are four main uses of the bracketing comma: (1) to set off nonessential information in the middle of a sentence; (2) to set off an opening phrase or clause; (3) to set off a closing phrase or clause; and (4) to set off speech in direct dialogue.

First, bracketing commas set off nonessential (nonrestrictive) information placed in the middle of a sentence. Such information (in the form of phrases and clauses) is not essential to the main idea of the sentence; in fact, we can test this. If after omitting words the sentence still makes sense, we know these words are nonessential and optional.

| Correct | *The Tale of Genji*, written in the eleventh century, is considered by literary historians to be the world's first novel. |
|---|---|

The main idea is that *The Tale of Genji* is considered to be the world's first novel. The intervening phrase, "written in the eleventh century," merely introduces additional but nonessential information.

| Correct | The old brick house that is painted yellow is now a historical landmark. |
|---|---|
| Correct | The old brick house at O'Claire Point, which we visited last year, is now a historical landmark. |

Regarding the first of two examples at the bottom of the previous page, "that is painted yellow" defines which old brick house the author is discussing. In the second example, the main point is that the old brick house at O'Claire Point is now a historical landmark, and the intervening clause "which we visited last year" merely adds additional but nonessential information.

The second major use of the bracketing comma is to set off opening phrases and clauses from the main sentence (independent clause).

| | |
|---|---|
| Correct | Like those of Sir Isaac Newton, the scientific contributions of Albert Einstein have proven monumental. |
| | (A comma in the above sentence separates the prepositional phrase "like those of Sir Issac Newton" from the main sentence.) |
| Correct | Having collected rare coins for more than fifteen years, Bill was heartbroken when his collection was stolen in a house burglary. |
| | (A comma separates the participial phrase "having collected rare coins for more than fifteen years" from the main sentence. This participle (or participial) phrase serves as an adjective in describing Bill.) |

If the opening phrase is very short, the use of the comma is considered optional. In the following example, the decision whether to use a comma after "at present" rests with the writer.

| | |
|---|---|
| Correct | At present we are a crew of eight. |

The third major use, though not as common as the first two uses, involves bracketing a nonessential closing phrase or clause from the main sentence (independent clause).

Correct           I hope we can talk more about this idea during the conference, if time permits.

                       (A comma is used to set off the phrase "if time permits" because this phrase functions as a piece of nonessential information. If we deleted these words, the sentence would still make sense.)

Correct           They woke up at 6 a.m., when they heard the rooster crowing.

Correct           They woke up when they heard the rooster crowing.

                       (The first of the above two sentences contains a nonessential clause which is bracketed. The fact that "they woke up at 6 a.m." is the critical information. The reason for their waking up is auxiliary information. However, in the second sentence, "when they heard the rooster crowing" is critical information about why they woke up. This restrictive information is <u>not</u> set off by commas.)

*NOTE* ∽ A point of possible confusion occurs when a sentence ends with a phrase or clause beginning with "which." For example: "I like that new brand of coffee, which is now on sale." It is common practice to place a comma before "which" because it is assumed that such closing phrases or clauses are parenthetical. That is, they do not contain defining or essential information and should therefore be preceded by a comma. It is also common practice not to place a comma before phrases or clauses beginning with the word "that" because it is assumed that such phrases or clauses do contain defining or essential information. However, the question remains, Is a comma really necessary, especially in this short sentence? One editing trick is to substitute "that" for "which" in order to edit out the comma (along with the word "which"). Nonetheless, for those who prefer to use "which" without the comma (at least in short sentences as in the example above), one rationale for doing so is the fact that these two words—"that" and "which"—are virtually interchangeable in meaning.

The fourth major use of the bracketing comma is to set off quoted speech from the speaker.

Correct          The waitress said, "See you next time."
                 "Thank you," we replied.

The same treatment is afforded to unspoken dialogue or "thought speech." Most commonly it is enclosed within quotation marks, but alternatively, it may be italicized to contrast it with actual speech.

Correct          "And what is the use of a book," thought Alice,
                 "without pictures or conversation?"

Correct          *And what is the use of a book without pictures or
                 conversation?*

It is not necessary to use both a speech tag (e.g., "thought Alice") and italics, since use of both techniques is redundant. Placing "thought speech" in quotation marks is common practice in nonfiction writing. Placing "thought speech" in italics is common practice in fiction writing.

Similar treatment is applied when setting off a quotation.

Correct          Was it Robert Frost who wrote, "Good fences
                 make good neighbors"?

One important distinction arises between the direct quotations and material that is merely surrounded by quotation marks. In the latter situation, we punctuate, with reference to commas, in exactly the same manner as we would "regular" sentences. This is also the same method used for punctuating sentences when dealing with sayings, maxims, adages, aphorisms, proverbs, or mottoes.

Correct          The statement "Some cats are mammals" necessarily implies that "Some mammals are cats."

                 (It's the writer's choice whether to capitalize the word "some.")

Correct          Our manager's favorite saying, "Rein in the nickels," is also his most annoying.

In the example above, commas are used because the saying "Rein in the nickels" is effectively nonessential information, the omission of which would still not destroy the sentence. Case in point: "Our manager's favorite saying is also his most annoying."

NOTE ⤌ Bracketing commas are, of course, used with dates, addresses, and salutations (opening lines of letters or memos) and complimentary closes. These uses are quite common and easily understood; they are not covered here as they are unlikely to cause confusion.

**Joining Comma**

Use commas to separate independent clauses connected by coordinating conjunctions such as *and, but, yet, or, nor, for,* and *so.* (Independent clauses are clauses that can stand alone as complete sentences.)

Correct          Susan wants to get her story published, and she wants to have it made into a movie.

Correct          Maurice ate habanero peppers with almost every meal, yet he hardly ever got indigestion.

The following is a potentially tricky situation in which it is difficult to determine whether the comma goes before or after the *and*.

Correct          I'll put together a business plan, and by next
                 week, I'll send it to a few potential investors.

In the previous example, there must be a joining comma before *and,* and ideally a bracketing comma after *week.* We have, after all, two complete sentences: "I'll put together a business plan" and "By next week, I'll send it to a few potential investors." Note that the comma before *and* cannot be a bracketing comma because we cannot remove the words "and by next week" without creating a run-on sentence (i.e., two sentences that are joined without proper punctuation). Note that we could put a comma after *and* (given that "by next week" is an optional phrase), but we typically do not as a matter of practice. Thus, in the next example below, the use of a third comma, although not visually pleasing, is not incorrect:

Correct          I'll put together a business plan, and, by next
                 week, I'll send it to a few potential investors.

Correct          Some experts do not believe alcoholism should
                 be called a disease and, moreover, believe
                 that any type of dependency can be cured by
                 identifying and treating its underlying causes.

In the previous example, we do not have two complete sentences, so we cannot have a joining comma (i.e., "believe that any type of dependency can be cured by identifying and treating its underlying causes" is not a complete sentence). But since the connecting word "moreover" is merely optional, it should be enclosed with commas. In other words, we could write: "Some experts do not believe alcoholism should be called a disease and believe that any type of dependency can be cured by identifying and treating its underlying causes." Knowing that we can omit a word or words and still have a sentence that makes sense is the telltale sign that we have an optional phrase.

A joining comma is optional in the case of two very short, complete sentences (independent clauses) joined by a coordinating conjunction.

Correct          The rain has stopped and the sun is shining.

Correct          The clouds are gone but it's windy.

The coordinating conjunctions "and" and "but" each join two complete sentences.

### Contrasting Comma

Correct          The new music director vowed to take an
                 active, not passive, fundraising role.

Correct          She didn't cry from sorrow and pain, but from
                 relief and joy.

In both of the above sentences, there is sufficiently strong contrast to warrant the use of a contrasting comma.

Correct          A poorer but happier man could not be found.

In the above example, however, no commas are used to bracket the words "but happier." The important point in deciding whether to use contrasting commas rests primarily with the emphasis needed within a given sentence. Strong emphasis will require commas to separate contrasting word groups; light to moderate emphasis will not require the aid of commas. The distinction regarding using or not using a pair of contrasting commas has little to nothing to do with whether the words are essential. It could be argued that all information is essential when using contrasting commas.

*NOTE* ✑ When "because" joins two parts of a sentence, does a comma go before the word "because"? This is a mystery question open to debate. Consider these two examples:

Correct          Don't forget to bring an umbrella because it's going to rain out.

Correct          To tell those grief-stricken people that we know how they feel is disingenuous, because we don't know how they feel.

Some writers like to place a comma before almost every use of "because." They would prefer to write, "Don't forget to bring an umbrella, because it's going to rain out." A likely better, more consistent, practice is to use a comma before "because" only if that comma qualifies as a contrasting comma, or perhaps a bracketing comma.

Case in point: There is not a strong sense of contrast between the need to remember to bring an umbrella given the likelihood of rain. There is, however, a stronger sense of contrast in thinking that we know how other grief-stricken people feel and the fact that we likely don't know how they feel. Most often, we will not require a comma before the word "because." First, use of the subordinating conjunction "because" creates a logical connection between ideas in a sentence, making it unlikely that the information it connects is nonessential (therefore no bracketing comma is needed). Second, the word "because" embodies a reasonable degree of contrast, obviating the need for a contrasting comma.

*NOTE* ✑ In practice, if a sentence is short, a contrasting comma is not used before the second component part of the correlative conjunction "not only...but (also)." Thus, in the following sentence, no comma would be used before "but": "Our apartment is not only cheap but centrally located." For longer sentences, it is common practice to use a comma before the second component part of the correlative conjunction. As such, a comma would likely be used before "but" in the following sentence: "For North Americans, natural gas is not only a cheaper and cleaner petroleum-based fuel, but also a readily available one."

Use a comma to separate word groups that flow in natural opposition to each other.

| | |
|---|---|
| Correct | Out of sight, out of mind. |
| Correct | The more you practice, the better you'll get. |

A contrasting comma is also used to separate two identical words in succession.

| | |
|---|---|
| Correct | This is a great, great ice-cream flavor. |
| Correct | Many, many articles have been written about weight loss and weight gain. |

### Omission Comma

Use commas to indicate missing words. In those situations involving adjectives, the missing word is typically *and*.

| | |
|---|---|
| Correct | I can't believe you sat through that long, dull, uninspired lecture without once checking your watch. |

We can test this sentence by replacing each comma with *and*:

| | |
|---|---|
| Correct | I can't believe you sat through that long and dull and uninspired lecture without once checking your watch. |
| Correct | It was a juicy, ripe mango. |
| Incorrect | It was a juicy ripe mango. |
| Incorrect | It was a juicy, ripe, mango. |

A comma is required to separate *juicy* from *ripe*. There are two ways to confirm this. First, substitute *and* for the comma and see if things still make sense. (Example: "It was a juicy and ripe mango.") Second, reverse the word order and see if the sentence makes sense. (Example: "It was a ripe, juicy mango.") Either or both of these tests confirm that a comma is needed.

A comma should not be placed after *ripe* because *and* cannot be substituted for it. For instance, the phrase "ripe and mango" makes no sense. The rule is that a comma should not be placed between the modifier and the noun it modifies.

A comma can be used to take the place of omitted words.

Correct          The first playoff game was exciting; the
                 second, dull.

In the above sentence, the comma takes the place of the "playoff game was." The sentence effectively reads: "The first playoff game was exciting; the second playoff game was dull."

### Confusion Comma

A comma may be used to prevent confusion, particularly in those situations where the absence of a comma would otherwise cause the reader to misread.

Incorrect        To Karen Jane was as heroic a real-life
                 character as could be found in any novel.

Correct          To Karen, Jane was as heroic a real-life
                 character as could be found in any novel.

The eye cannot resist reading both names together as if they represent a first and last name.

Incorrect        Run for your life is in danger.

Correct          Run, for your life is in danger.

One could argue that a contrasting comma is needed in the above example. However, the actual problem is that the reader's eye has trouble knowing how to group the words properly.

Incorrect        The speaker said: "On Day 1 I will discuss the reasons for the global increase in diabetes and on Day 2 I will talk about how to curtail this trend."

Correct          The speaker said: "On Day 1, I will discuss the reasons for the global increase in diabetes, and on Day 2, I will talk about how to curtail this trend."

Obviously, a comma is needed in the above example to avoid confusion between the close proximity of the numbers 1 and 2 and the personal pronoun "I."

## Exercise on Comma Usage

Correct the comma usage in each sentence by observing the five classic uses of commas: listing, bracketing, joining, contrasting, or omission. Answers can be found on pages 323–325.

1.   The Oscar the Emmy and the Tony are three related awards which confuse many people.

2.   Emerging from the ruins of the World War II Japan embarked on an economic recovery that can be only viewed in historical terms as astonishing.

3.   Every major band requires, a lead singer, a lead guitarist, a bass guitarist, and a drummer.

4.   A dedicated empathetic individual can achieve lifetime recognition as a United Nations worker.

5.   More than a few people were shocked to discover that a torn, previously worn, pair of Madonna's underwear sold for more money at auction than did a large, splendid, sketch by Vignon.

6.   The more he talked with her the more he liked her.

7.   The crowded housing tenement, a cluster of rundown, look-alike apartments was the site of the Prime Minister's birthplace.

8.   South Africa is famous for her gold and diamonds, Thailand, for her silk and emeralds, and Brazil for her coffee and sugarcane.

9.   She reached for the clock, and finding it, hastily silenced the alarm.

10.   Josie originally wanted to be a nurse but after finishing university she decided to become a flight attendant instead.

## Mastering Semicolons

Use a semicolon instead of a coordinating conjunction (that is, *and, but, yet, or, nor, for, so*) to link two closely related sentences. The key thing to remember is that a semicolon separates complete sentences. It is not used if one or more of those sentences is a fragment.

| | |
|---|---|
| Correct | Today's students are more creative and technologically savvy, but they are also weaker in the basics of reading, writing, and arithmetic. |
| Correct | Today's students are more creative and technologically savvy; they are also weaker in the basics of reading, writing, and arithmetic. |

Use a semicolon between independent clauses connected by words such as *however, therefore, moreover, nevertheless,* and *consequently.* These special words are called conjunctive adverbs.

| | |
|---|---|
| Incorrect | The formulas for many scientific discoveries appear rudimentary, however, when one examines a derivation behind these formulas they do not seem so rudimentary after all. |
| Correct | The formulas for many scientific discoveries appear rudimentary; however, when one examines a derivation behind these formulas they do not seem so rudimentary after all. |

## Avoiding Run-on Sentences

To see commas and semicolons in action, let's review a very common error—the run-on sentence. A run-on refers to two sentences that are inappropriately joined together, usually by a comma. There are effectively four ways to correct a run-on sentence, as seen in each of the four correct options below. First, join the two sentences with a semicolon. Second, join the two sentences with a coordinating conjunction (e.g., *and, but, yet, or, nor, for, so*). Third, separate the two sentences with a period. Fourth, turn one of the two sentences into a subordinate clause.

| | |
|---|---|
| Incorrect | Technology has made our lives easier, it has also made our lives more complicated. |
| Correct | Technology has made our lives easier; it has also made our lives more complicated. |
| | (This solution involves changing the comma to a semicolon.) |
| Correct | Technology has made our lives easier, and it has also made our lives more complicated. |
| | (This solution involves joining two sentences with a coordinating conjunction.) |
| Correct | Technology has made our lives easier. It has also made our lives more complicated. |
| | (This solution involves making two separate sentences.) |
| Correct | Even though technology has made our lives easier, it has also made our lives more complicated. |
| | (This solution involves turning one sentence into a subordinate clause. Here the focus is on the idea that technology has made our lives more complicated (independent clause). The subordinate idea is that it has made our lives easier (subordinate clause). It would also be equally correct to say: "Even though technology has made our lives more complicated, it has also made our lives easier." Now the central idea and subordinate idea are reversed.) |

## Answers to the Exercise on Comma Usage

1.  The Oscar, the Emmy, and the Tony are three related awards which confuse many people.

    The comma after Emmy is required in American English but omitted in British English.

2.  Emerging from the ruins of the World War II, Japan embarked on an economic recovery that can only be viewed in historical terms as astonishing.

    A bracketing comma is required after "World War II."

3.  Every major band requires a lead singer, a lead guitarist, a bass guitarist, and a drummer.

    There should be no comma after the verb "requires."

4.  A dedicated, empathetic individual can achieve lifetime recognition as a United Nations worker.

    An omission comma separates "dedicated and empathetic." There are two ways to test for this. First, substitute the word "and" to read "dedicated and empathetic." Second, reverse the order of the two words to read "empathetic, dedicated individual." Since either substituting the word "and" or reversing the word order still makes sense in context, a comma should be used.

5.  More than a few people were shocked to discover that a torn, previously worn pair of Madonna's underwear sold for more money at the auction than did a large, splendid sketch by Vignon.

    There are no commas after "previously worn" or "sketch." A comma is not placed between a modifier and the word it modifies. Here the words being modified are a "pair of Madonna's underwear" and "sketch."

6.     The more he talked with her, the more he liked her.

A contrasting comma after "her" is required.

7.     That crowded housing tenement, a cluster of run-down, look-alike apartments, was the site of the Prime Minister's birthplace.

Insert a comma after "apartments"; the phrase "a cluster of run-down, look-alike apartments" is nonessential (and therefore optional) and should be enclosed with commas.

8.     South Africa is famous for her gold and diamonds, Thailand, for her silk and emeralds, and Brazil, for her coffee and sugarcane.

A comma is needed after Thailand and Brazil. Such a comma (an omission comma) takes the place of the words "is famous." So, the sentence effectively reads: "South Africa is famous for her gold and diamonds, Thailand is famous for her silk and emeralds, and Brazil is famous for her coffee and sugarcane."

There are at least two additional ways to correct this sentence:

i)     By omitting the second comma in the original:

"South Africa is famous for her gold and diamonds, Thailand for her silk and emeralds, and Brazil for her coffee and sugarcane."

The treatment is consistent with the rules of ellipsis. We can acceptably omit words (in this case the words "is famous") when they are readily understood in context.

ii)   By using semicolons with commas:

"South Africa is famous for her gold and diamonds; Thailand, for her silk and emeralds; and Brazil, for her coffee and sugarcane."

Semicolons can be used in conjunction with commas, especially in cases of heavily punctuated sentences. The final "and" appearing before "Brazil" is optional.

9.   She reached for the clock and, finding it, hastily silenced the alarm.

A bracketing comma is needed before and after the words "finding it"; this is a nonessential phrase. Removing these words still results in a complete sentence. Case in point: "She reached for the clock and hastily silenced the alarm." If, however, we were to remove the words "and finding it," the sentence would become nonsensical: "She reached for the clock hastily silenced the alarm." Therefore this confirms that a set of bracketing commas cannot be used in the original sentence.

10.   Josie originally wanted to be a nurse, but after finishing university, she decided to become a flight attendant instead.

A joining comma is required before "but," while a bracketing comma is required after "university." We effectively have two sentences: "Josie originally wanted to be a nurse" and "After finishing university, she decided to become a flight attendant." In the solution above, the two commas do not both function as bracketing commas; if this were so we could cut out the phrase "but after finishing university" and the sentence would still make sense, but it doesn't: "Josie originally wanted to be a nurse she decided to become a flight attendant instead."

## Appendix IV — American English vs. British English

American English and British English are the two major engines behind the evolving English language. Other English-speaking countries—most notably Canada, Australia, New Zealand, India, the Philippines, and South Africa—embrace a variant of one or both of these two major systems. Although American and British English do not differ with respect to grammar per se, each system has its own peculiarities in terms of spelling and punctuation. The purpose of this section is to provide a snapshot of these differences.

## Spelling Differences

**Spelling fine points.** The British generally double the final *-l* when adding suffices that begin with a vowel, where Americans double it only on stressed syllables. This makes sense given that American English treats *-l* the same as other final consonants, whereas British English treats it as an exception. For example, whereas Americans spell *counselor, equaling, modeling, quarreled, signaling, traveled,* and *tranquility,* the British spell *counsellor, equalling, modelling, quarrelled, signalling, travelled,* and *tranquillity.*

Certain words—*compelled, excelling, propelled,* and *rebelling*—are spelled the same on both platforms, consistent with the fact that the British double the *-l* while Americans observe the stress on the second syllable. The British also use a single *-l* before suffixes beginning with a consonant, whereas Americans use a double *-l*. Thus, the British spell *enrolment, fulfilment, instalment,* and *skilful,* Americans spell *enrollment, fulfillment, installment,* and *skillful.*

Deciding which nouns and verbs end in *-ce* or *-se* is understandably confusing. In general, nouns in British English are spelled *-ce* (e.g., *defence, offence, pretence*) while nouns in American English are spelled *-se* (e.g., *defense, offense, pretense*). Moreover, American and British English retain the noun-verb distinction in which the noun is spelled with *-ce* and the core verb is spelled with an *-se*. Examples include: *advice* (noun), *advise* (verb), *advising* (verb) and *device* (noun), *devise* (verb), *devising* (verb).

With respect to *licence* and *practice,* the British uphold the noun-verb distinction for both words: *licence* (noun), *license* (verb), *licensing* (verb) and *practice* (noun), *practise* (verb), *practising* (verb). Americans, however, spell *license* with a *-s* across the board: *license* (noun), *license* (verb), *licensing* (verb), although *licence* is an accepted variant spelling for the noun form. Americans further spell *practice* with a *-c* on all accounts: *practice* (noun), *practice* (verb), *practicing* (verb).

## CHART OF SPELLING DIFFERENCES BETWEEN AMERICAN ENGLISH AND BRITISH ENGLISH

| American English | | British English | |
|---|---|---|---|
| -ck | check | -que | cheque |
| -ed | learned | -t | learnt |
| -er | center, meter | -re | centre, metre |
| -no e | judgment, acknowledgment | -e | judgement, acknowledgement |
| -no st | among, amid | -st | amongst, amidst |
| -in | inquiry | -en | enquiry |
| -k | disk | -c | disc |
| -l | traveled, traveling | -ll | travelled, travelling |
| -ll | enroll, fulfillment | -l | enrol, fulfilment |
| -m | program | -mme | programme |
| -o | mold, smolder | -ou | mould, smoulder |
| -og | catalog | -ogue | catalogue |
| -or | color, favor | -our | colour, favour |
| -s | defense, offense | -c | defence, offence |
| -z | summarize, organization | -s | summarise, organisation |

## Punctuation Differences

The following serves to highlight some of major differences in punctuation between America English and British English.

### Abbreviations

| American English | British English |
|---|---|
| Mr. / Mrs. / Ms. | Mr / Mrs / Ms |

Americans use a period (full stop) after salutations; the British do not.

| American English | British English |
|---|---|
| Nadal vs. Federer | Nadal v. Federer |

Americans use "vs." for versus; the British write "v." for versus. Note that Americans also use the abbreviation v. in legal contexts. For example, Gideon v. Wainright.

### Colons

| American English | British English |
|---|---|
| We found the place easily: Your directions were perfect. | We found the place easily: your directions were perfect. |

Americans often capitalize the first word after a colon, if what follows is a complete sentence. The British prefer not to capitalize the first word that follows the colon, even if what follows is a full sentence.

## Commas

| American English | British English |
| --- | --- |
| She likes the sun, sand, and sea. | She likes the sun, sand and sea. |

Americans use a comma before the "and" or "or" when listing a series of items. The British do not use a comma before the "and" when listing a series of items.

| American English | British English |
| --- | --- |
| In contact sports (e.g., American football and rugby) physical strength and weight are of obvious advantage. | In contact sports (e.g. American football and rugby) physical strength and weight are of obvious advantage. |

The abbreviation "i.e." stands for "that is"; the abbreviation "e.g." stands for "for example." In American English, a comma always follows the second period in each abbreviation (when the abbreviation is used in context). In British English, a comma is never used after the second period in either abbreviation.

Note that under both systems, these abbreviations are constructed with two periods, one after each letter. The following variant forms are *not* correct under either system: "eg.," or "eg." or "ie.," or "ie."

## Dashes

| American English | British English |
|---|---|
| The University of Bologna – the oldest university in the Western World – awarded its first degree in 1088. | The University of Bologna - the oldest university in the Western World - awarded its first degree in 1088. |

The British have traditionally favored the use of a hyphen where Americans have favored the use of the dash. Discussion of the two types of dashes is found in *Appendix II – Editing Tune-up*.

## Quotation Marks

| American English | British English |
|---|---|
| Some see education as a "vessel to be filled," others see it as a "fire to be lit." | Some see education as a 'vessel to be filled', others see it as a 'fire to be lit'. |

Americans use double quotation marks. The British typically use single quotation marks.

| American English | British English |
|---|---|
| Our boss said, "The customer is never wrong." | Our boss said, 'The customer is never wrong.' |
| Or: "The customer is never wrong," our boss said. | Or: 'The customer is never wrong,' our boss said. |

Periods and commas are placed inside quotation marks in American English (almost without exception). In British English, the treatment is twofold. Punctuation goes inside quotation marks if it's part of the quote itself; if not, quotation marks go on the outside. This means that in British English periods and commas go on the outside of quotation marks in all situations not involving dialogue or direct speech. However, in situations involving direct speech, periods and commas generally go inside of quotation marks because they are deemed to be part of the dialogue itself.

*NOTE* ✦ Today, the practice of using single quotation marks is not ubiquitous in the United Kingdom. A number of UK-based newspapers, publishers, and media companies now follow the practice of using double quotation marks.

## Appendix V – Traditional Writing vs. Digital Writing

There are two different platforms across which writing takes place—traditional, paper-based and electronic, digital-based. Three questions may arise when writing for these two different media: Should writing across different platforms be different, and if so, how is it different and what dynamics cause this difference? The debate over whether there should be a difference in terms of writing standards is essentially a values debate to which there is no correct answer. However, from a practical standpoint, there is little doubt that written communication across these media differs and will remain different.

## Formal Writing vs. Informal Writing

The dynamics that cause a difference between traditional and digital writing center on the distinction between static and non-static written communication. Electronic communication arguably exists to take the place of spoken communication, and to that extent, it is non-static, tending to be more conversational and less structured.

Traditional or paper-based writing is most often associated with formal writing, while electronic or digital-based writing is commonly the domain of informal writing. As mentioned, traditional writing overlaps in large degree with formal writing. Formal writing, loosely defined, is writing consisting of multiple paragraphs that is meant to be distributed and read by one or more persons. Examples of formal written documents include long e-mails, letters, newsletters, news articles, brochures, essays, reports, manuals, and books.

Digital writing dovetails with informal writing. Examples of digital writing include short personal and business e-mails, text messaging, blogging, and messaging on social network sites such as MySpace, Facebook, and Twitter.

How do the different forms of written communication stack up in terms of their likely level of written formality? As briefly summarized next, the higher the technological level, the more informal writing tends to be. Naturally, this analysis embodies a degree of generality. Blogging, for example, can be quite formal, as is the case with blog articles published by the Huffington Post. Most blog responses, however, tend to be as informal as are casual e-mails or text messaging.

*Writing—Levels of Informality*

| Level | Examples |
| --- | --- |
| Fifth level | text messaging, instant messaging (for example, Yahoo, Skype), and microblogging (Twitter) |
| Fourth level | blogging, e-mails |
| Third level | letter writing, articles, newsletters, brochures, websites, memos, flyers, slide shows |
| Second level | manuals, business reports, academic essays |
| First level | published documents such as reports, newspapers, magazines, and books |

## Stylistic Differences with Online Writing

Some of the telltale signs of informality in the digital realm (for better or worse) include the following: shorter sentences; optional punctuation, including non-capitalized words and abbreviated spelling; the use of fewer adjectives and adverbs; the frequent use of ellipses, asterisks, and exclamation points; and the occasional use of smileys and e-mail acronyms.

Many traditionalists object to the use of abbreviated spelling and non-capitalization. For example, dashing off "c u @12 - lunch" translates as "see you at 12 o'clock for lunch." But consider the level of informality. Assuming this to be a text message, the message, once sent and received, will never be seen again. So what purpose would it serve to make it more formal?

Such informality in written communication may be acceptable for text messaging, but it is considered unacceptable when used in standard expository writing. The point here is that although there is real logic as to why writing may be informal, this does not mean that informal writing is superior to formal writing because it is more practical, less structured, or somehow more authentic. Formal and informal writing are different and serve different purposes.

Also, many readers understand only the most basic smileys and e-mail acronyms. Certain e-mail acronyms are easy to understand—FYI ("For Your Information"), IMHO ("In My Humble/Honest Opinion"), and LOL ("Laughing Out Loud"). But where is the line of readability to be drawn? The average e-mail user would have a devil of a time deciphering each of the following: FYEO (For Your Eyes Only), PMFJI (Pardon Me For Jumping In), and IITYWYBMAD? (If I Tell You Will You Buy Me A Drink?). The same situation holds true for smileys (emoticons), for which actual Smiley Dictionaries exist. Smileys are read by turning the head counterclockwise and looking at them sideways; then the little faces can by seen. Most readers understand :-), ;-), and :-( to mean "I'm happy/it's funny," "winking/I think I'm being funny," and "I'm sad/it's sad." But other smileys are enigmatic for the uninitiated, notably: ;-\ (undecided), :-< (very upset), and :-# (my lips are sealed).

Certain writing techniques used in digital communications occur because typographical tools are limited or unavailable. Basic e-mail, for instance, doesn't provide a way to italicize or underline. And underlining of digital text should be avoided, as it is reserved for use as hyperlinks. In order to place emphasis on certain words and phrases, it is common practice to place them in asterisks or, occasionally, to capitalize them. An employee who e-mails, "You won't believe how *smoothly* our morning meeting went," is drawing attention to the word "smoothly" for the purpose of infusing a little sarcasm, as if things hadn't gone so smoothly after all.

The way information is read on the Internet influences how it is written. Individuals don't read information online as linearly as they do in printed formats. They tend to skip around, skimming and scanning, then stopping to read chunks of information.

How does this affect the way information is written for the web? Columns tend to be narrower (usually not more than seventy-five characters per line), sentences and paragraphs tend to be shorter, more heads and subheads are used to assist the reader in "grabbing" information, and more bolding is commonly used (both in black and in color).

## Benefits

In conclusion, the higher the standard one adheres to in all written communication, be it digital or print, the higher will be one's perceived level of professionalism. The cost is time and effort; the benefit is quality. Each individual must make his or her own "call." As the English language continues to evolve, with the digital revolution playing a significant role in this evolution, there will always exist a place for "good" writing. Writing that is strong in content, and equally adheres to currently accepted principles and rules—including grammar, spelling, and punctuation—will continue to have a positive influence on its readers.

# Selected Bibliography

*The Chicago Manual of Style*. 15th ed. Chicago: University of Chicago Press, 2003.

Clark, Roy Peter. *Writing Tools: 50 Essential Strategies for Every Writer*. New York: Little, Brown and Company, 2008.

Cook, Claire Kehrwald. *Line by Line: How to Edit Your Own Writing*. Boston: Houghton Mifflin, 1985.

Ehrenhaft, George. *Barron's SAT Writing Workbook*. 2nd ed, Barron's Educational Series. Hauppage, NY: Barron's, 2009.

*Encarta Webster's Dictionary of the English Language*. 2nd ed. New York: Bloomsbury, 2004.

Fogarty, Mignon. "Grammar Girl: Quick and Dirty Tips for Better Writing." http://grammar.quickanddirtytips.com/.

Fogiel, Max. *The English Handbook of Grammar, Style, and Composition*. Piscataway, NJ: Research and Education Association, 1987.

King, Stephen. *On Writing: A Memoir of the Craft*. New York: Pocket Books, 2000.

Kramer, Melinda, Glenn H. Leggett, and C. David Mead. *Prentice Hall Handbook for Writers*. 11th ed. Englewood Cliffs, NJ: Prentice Hall, 1995.

*Merriam Webster's Collegiate Dictionary*. 11th ed. Springfield, MA: Merriam Webster, 2005.

Opdycke, John B. *Harper's English Grammar*. New York: Warner, 1983.

*Oxford Dictionary of English*. 2nd ed. New York: Oxford University Press, 2005.

Ritter, Robert M. *The Oxford Style Manual.* New York: Oxford University Press, 2003.

Skillin, Marjorie E., and Robert M. Gay. *Words into Type.* 3rd ed. Englewood Cliffs, NJ: Prentice-Hall, 1974.

Strunk, William, Jr., and E. B. White. *The Elements of Style.* 4th ed. New York: Allyn and Bacon, 2000.

Trask, Robert Lawrence. *The Penguin Guide to Punctuation.* London: Penguin, 1999.

Truss, Lynne. *Eats, Shoots & Leaves: The Zero Tolerance Approach to Punctuation.* New York: Gotham, 2004.

Venolla, Jan. *Write Right! A Desktop Digest of Punctuation, Grammar, and Style.* 4th ed. Berkeley: Ten Speed Press, 2004.

Warriner, John E. *English Composition and Grammar: Complete Course.* Orlando, FL: Harcourt Brace Jovanovich, 1988.

*Wikipedia, The Free Encyclopedia,* s.v. "Writing Style," http://en.wikipedia.org/wiki/Writing_style.

Wilbers, Stephen. *Keys to Great Writing.* Cincinnati, OH: Writer's Digest Books, 2000. Reprinted in paperback, 2007.

Williams, Joseph M. *Style: Toward Clarity and Grace.* Chicago: University of Chicago Press, 1995.

Winokur, Jon. *Advice to Writers: A Compendium of Quotes, Anecdotes, and Writerly Wisdom from a Dazzling Array of Literary Lights.* New York: Vintage, 2000.

Zinsser, William. *On Writing Well: 30th Anniversary Edition: The Classic Guide to Writing Nonfiction.* New York: Harper Paperbacks, 2006.

# Index

Numbers in *italics* (within brackets) indicate multiple-choice problems, 1 to 30. They are preceded by corresponding page numbers.

# About the Author

Brandon Royal is an award-winning writer whose educational authorship includes *The Little Red Writing Book, The Little Gold Grammar Book, The Little Blue Reasoning Book,* and *The Little Green Math Book.* During his tenure working in Hong Kong for US-based Kaplan Educational Centers—a Washington Post subsidiary and the largest test-preparation organization in the world—Brandon honed his theories of teaching and education and developed a set of key learning "principles" to help define the basics of writing, grammar, math, and reasoning.

A Canadian by birth and graduate of the University of Chicago's Booth School of Business, his interest in writing began after completing writing courses at Harvard University. Since then he has authored a dozen books and reviews of his books have appeared in *Time Asia* magazine, *Publishers Weekly, Library Journal of America, Midwest Book Review, The Asian Review of Books, Choice Reviews Online, Asia Times Online,* and About.com.

Brandon is a five-time winner of the International Book Awards, a seven-time gold medalist at the President's Book Awards, as well as recipient of the "Educational Book of the Year" award as presented by the Book Publishers Association of Alberta. He has also been a winner or finalist at the Ben Franklin Book Awards, the Global eBook Awards, the Beverly Hills Book Awards, the IPPY Awards, the USA Book News "Best Book Awards," and the *Foreword* magazine Book of the Year Awards. He continues to write and publish in the belief that there will always be a place for books that inspire, enlighten, and enrich.

To contact the author:
E-mail: contact@brandonroyal.com
Web site: www.brandonroyal.com

**Books by Brandon Royal**

*The Little Blue Reasoning Book:*
  *50 Powerful Principles for Clear and Effective Thinking*

*The Little Red Writing Book:*
  *20 Powerful Principles for Clear and Effective Writing*

*The Little Gold Grammar Book:*
  *40 Powerful Rules for Clear and Correct Writing*

*The Little Red Writing Book Deluxe Edition:*
  *Two Winning Books in One, Writing plus Grammar*

*The Little Green Math Book:*
  *30 Powerful Principles for Building Math and Numeracy Skills*

*The Little Purple Probability Book:*
  *Master the Thinking Skills to Succeed in Basic Probability*

*Ace the GMAT:*
  *Master the GMAT in 40 Days*

*Getting into Business School:*
  *100 Proven Admissions Strategies to Get You Accepted at the*
  *MBA Program of Your Choice*

*Dancing for Your Life:*
  *The True Story of Maria de la Torre and Her Secret Life*
  *in a Hong Kong Go-Go Bar*

*The Map Maker:*
  *An Illustrated Short Story About How Each of Us Sees the*
  *World Differently and Why Objectivity is Just an Illusion*

*Paradise Island:*
  *A Dreamer's Guidebook on How to Survive Paradise and*
  *Triumph over Human Nature*

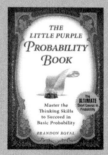

CPSIA information can be obtained
at www.ICGtesting.com
Printed in the USA
BVOW11s0406070717
488550BV00006B/95/P